Illustrator:
Karon Walstad
Sue Fullam

Editor:
Janet Cain, M.Ed.

Editorial Project Manager:
Ina Massler Levin, M.A.

Editor-in-Chief:
Sharon Coan, M.S. Ed.

Art Director:
Elayne Roberts

Associate Designer:
Denise Bauer

Cover Artist:
Sue Fullam

Product Manager:
Phil Garcia

Imaging:
Hillary Merriman

Publishers:
Rachelle Cracchiolo, M.S. Ed.
Mary Dupuy Smith, M.S. Ed.

Early Childhood Units
for
MUSIC

Author:

Ruth Bergad

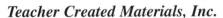

Teacher Created Materials, Inc.
6421 Industry Way
Westminster, CA 92683
www.teachercreated.com

©1995 Teacher Created Materials, Inc.
Reprinted, 2002

Made in U.S.A.
ISBN-1-55734-205-9

Table of Contents

Introduction

Early Childhood Units for Music is a 144-page resource book for use in the early childhood classroom. It provides specific strategies and activities for integrating music into the early childhood curriculum. Connecting curriculum areas is a popular trend in education with the goal of building literacy while enhancing students' interest and making learning more meaningful. By using quality musical selections with related activities, students will increase their proficiency in spoken and written language, learn new concepts, improve their self-concepts, and learn to appreciate the world of music.

This book extends and reinforces concepts and forms of expression from several curriculum areas. Activities include:

Art	Cooking	Critical Thinking	Reproducible Little Books
Drama	Games	Culminating Activities	Flannel Board Patterns
Poetry	Science	Writing	Brainstorming
Math	Center Ideas	Language Arts	Sample Lesson Plans

Activities may be chosen to fit the needs of your classroom and your teaching style.

Introduction *(cont.)*

Why Whole-Language?

A whole-language approach involves students in using all modes of communication: reading, writing, listening, observing, illustrating, experiencing, and doing. Communication skills are interconnected and integrated into lessons that emphasize the whole of language rather than isolating its parts. The lessons revolve around music selections. Reading is not taught as a separate subject from writing and spelling, for example. A student reads, writes (spelling appropriately for his/her level), speaks, listens, etc., in response to a musical experience introduced by the teacher. In this way, language skills grow naturally, stimulated by involvement and interest in the topic at hand.

Why Thematic Planning?

One very useful tool for implementing an integrated whole-language program is thematic planning. By choosing a specific theme, a teacher can plan activities throughout the day that lead to a cohesive, in-depth study of the topic. Students will be practicing and applying their skills in meaningful contexts. Consequently, they will tend to learn and retain more. Both teachers and students will be freed from a day that is broken into unrelated segments of isolated drill and practice.

Why Cooperative Learning?

Besides academic skills and content, students need to learn social skills. No longer can this area of development be taken for granted. Students must learn to work cooperatively in groups in order to function well in modern society. Group activities should be a regular part of school life, and teachers should consciously include social objectives as well as academic objectives in their planning. For example, a group working together to write a report may need to select a leader. The teacher should make clear to the students and monitor the qualities of good leader-follower group interaction just as he/she would state and monitor the academic goals of the project.

Why Music?

Music is an important part of everyday life. Activities related to musical selections give students opportunities to listen, sing, play instruments, experience rhythm through movement, and creatively express themselves. A wide variety of academic, physical, and social skills can be taught and reinforced through the use of music. In addition, students learn to appreciate the similarities and differences among cultures when they are introduced to music from around the world. Music is truly a universal language that can be used to enrich the lives of all students.

Unit Preparation

Prepare the materials necessary for teaching *Early Childhood Units for Music*. Some general suggestions are given below.

Gathering Materials: Go to your school or public library to locate books that relate to the theme. See the bibliography (page 144) for suggestions. Obtain recordings of the featured musical selections from the music specialist at your school, the public library, or local music stores. Read the sample lesson plans to see what materials are needed for the activities in each unit.

Viewing Instruments: Whenever possible, display real instruments for students to examine. Check with local music stores to see if you can borrow instruments to show to your class. Try to arrange for musicians to bring and play their instruments or take a field trip to a rehearsal by a local symphony, high school band, etc.

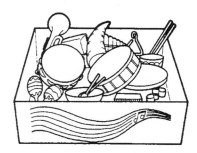

Sending Parent Letters: There are two parent letters, one relating to musical instruments and the other relating to composers. Reproduce and send home each letter as indicated in the sample lesson plans.

Using the Poetry: You may wish to copy the poems by making overhead transparencies, printing them on chart paper, or printing them on sentence strips. Individual copies of the poems can be kept in a poetry folder.

Making Little Books: Reproduce the pages of the little books. Books may be assembled before the lesson, or students may help complete the following steps: 1. Cut on the dotted lines. 2. Check to make sure the pages are in the right order. 3. Staple the pages together. 4. Students may use crayons or markers to color their little books. 5. The books should be read together as a class, partners can take turns reading them to each other, and then the books can be taken home to share with family members.

Using Activity Pages: Reproduce appropriate activity pages for students. Directions for using the pages are given in the sample lesson plans.

Using the Patterns: Patterns are provided with many of the units. Trace these patterns on felt or Pellon 930 for use on a flannel board. Some patterns may be enlarged, traced on tagboard, and laminated for use in various center activities or on bulletin boards. The patterns can also be used to make stick puppets or props for retelling stories.

Setting Up Classroom Centers

Many different types of centers are appropriate in a whole-language classroom. The following are suggestions for types of centers and the materials needed in them.

Reading Center: fiction and nonfiction books, poetry books, magazines, Big Books, little books, student-created books, word charts, pocket chart, flannel board, sentence strips, chart paper, overhead projector, comfortable chairs, pillows, rugs

Listening Center: tape recorder and headphones, copies and tapes of the little books, and recordings of the featured musical selections

Writing Center: different types of paper, pencils, washable markers, crayons, alphabet stamps, wooden letters, magnetic letters and board, word-bank posters, pictionaries, typewriter, a computer with a simple word-processing program, blank journals, and books

Social Studies Center: globes, maps, pictures of musical instruments from around the world, pictures showing how different cultures make and use music

Math Center: a flannel board, number stamps, wooden numbers, magnetic numbers and board, an estimating jar, pattern blocks, small cubes, tangrams, small objects for counting (such as plastic teddy bears), a floor graph, a balance scale

Science Center: observation journals, posters and pictures, science books (both picture books and informational texts) about sound, a variety of equipment (such as tuning forks) for experimenting with sound

Art Center: white and colored paper of various sizes and textures, paints, crayons, markers, colored chalk, clay, glitter, tissue paper, old magazines, and fabric scraps

Dramatic Play Center: child-sized furniture; clothes and props for students to pretend being composers, conductors, and musicians; pictures of instruments

Music Center: a variety of musical instruments (including homemade instruments)

Experimenting with Sound

Use one or more of the activities shown below or on page 7 to give students the opportunity to experiment with sound. You may wish to use these activities to set the stage for *Early Childhood Units for Music* or to teach science concepts when using the featured musical selections.

I. Making Sound Visible

Place a piece of thick plastic so that it completely covers the top of a plastic bowl. Use a wide rubber band to secure the plastic in place. Be sure the plastic is stretched flat across the top of the bowl. Then tape down the sides of the plastic to the bowl. Put the bowl on a flat surface, and place some grains of uncooked rice on the piece of plastic. Hold a pan close to the top of the bowl. Bang a wooden spoon on the back of the pan. Students should observe the rice move as you hit the pan. Sound waves from the pan cause the plastic to vibrate and the rice to move.

II. Cup Communication

Obtain two plastic cups, and poke one small hole in the bottom of each. Cut 30 feet (9 m) of string. Thread one end of the string through the hole in one cup. Tie a large knot in the end of the string so that it will not pull out of the cup. Thread the other end of the string through the hole in the second cup. Tie a large knot there, too. Have pairs of students work together to communicate using the cups. One student from each pair should hold the cup up to his/her ear to listen while the partner holds the other cup up to his/her mouth and speaks. Ask students to take turns speaking and listening .

III. A Tuning Fork

Show students how a tuning fork works. Invite them to strike the tuning fork against a variety of objects to see how it sounds. Then hit the tuning fork against the top of a desk or table. Gently place the tuning fork so that the base touches a volunteer's head. Ask the student to describe how the tuning fork sounds. It should sound louder, since the bones in a person's head transmit the sound vibrations to the ears better than the air does. Allow other volunteers to listen to the tuning fork through their heads.

Experimenting with Sound *(cont.)*

IV. Bouncing Sounds

Create two stacks of books that are the same height. Place a cardboard tube, such as those used for toilet paper, on top of each stack. Be sure the cardboard tubes are lying on their sides and form a V shape. Position a watch or timer that ticks, at the end of a tube. Ask a volunteer to listen at the end of the other tube. Ask the volunteer if he/she can hear the ticking sound through the tube. The student will not be able to hear the ticking sound. Hold a plate at the bottom of the V, and ask the  volunteer to listen once again. This time the student will be able to hear the ticking sound because the sound waves are bouncing off of the plate into the second tube.

V. Sticks and Stones

Discuss safety rules before allowing students to handle the sticks and stones. Provide a variety of sticks and stones for students to use when experimenting with sounds. Have students tap together small stones, large stones, smooth stones, rough stones, long sticks, short sticks, smooth sticks, rough sticks, and different combinations of stones and sticks. Ask them to describe whether the sounds are louder or softer and higher or lower when tapping together the different types of sticks and stones. Allow students to create simple rhythms by tapping the sticks and/or stones. Invite volunteers to imitate the rhythms.

VI. Identifying Direction

Blindfold one student. Ask four or five other students to stand at a distance in a circle around the blindfolded student. Begin by having one student in the circle make sounds such as whistling, snapping fingers, or speaking softly. Ask the blindfolded student to identify the direction of the sounds. Continue the activity by asking the other students in the circle to make sounds and having the blindfolded student identify the direction of the sounds. Use additional volunteers and repeat this activity several times. You may wish to place a cotton ball in one ear of the blindfolded student. Discuss how the cotton ball affects the blindfolded student's ability to identify the direction of the sounds.

Sample Lesson Plans

Days 1 and 2: Create a bulletin board using pictures of different instruments. Send home copies of pages 9–10, 12–15, 17–20, 22–25, and 30–31 with the letter (page 138) telling parents that your class is studying about instruments, as well as composers, musicians, and conductors. Encourage family members to share their musical talents with your class (page 140). Reproduce pages 9 and 10 for students. Introduce the string instruments (violin, viola, violoncello, double bass). Have students make violins and bows (page 11).

Days 3 and 4: Reproduce pages 12–15 and 17–20 for students. Introduce the woodwind (flute, piccolo, oboe, English horn, clarinet, bass clarinet, bassoon, saxophone) and the brass instruments (trumpet, cornet, trombone, flügelhorn, tuba, sousaphone, French horn, baritone horn). Have students make flutes (page 16) and horns (page 21). You may wish to have students make clarinets from paper drinking straws. Help each student make a straw clarinet using the following directions: Pinch and flatten one end of the straw. Cut off the corners of the pinched end of the straw. Use a needle or pin to poke five holes in the straw. Be sure there is about one inch (2.54 cm) between the holes. Use a pencil or pen point to slightly enlarge the holes.

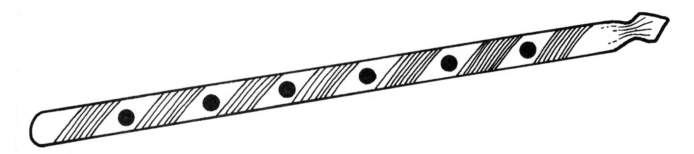

Days 5 and 6: Reproduce pages 22–25 for students. Introduce the percussion instruments (kettledrum, snare drum, bass drum, cymbals, triangle, xylophone, chimes, tambourine). Have students make drums (page 26), xylophones (page 27), tambourines (page 28), and cymbals (page 29).

Days 7 and 8: Reproduce pages 30 and 31 for students. Introduce the guitar, banjo, harp, and piano. Have students make harps (pages 32 and 33) and banjos (page 34). Have students draw themselves playing their favorite instruments (page 35).

Days 9 and 10: Make an overhead transparency or bulletin board to show students one possible seating arrangement for a symphony orchestra (page 36). Introduce composers, conductors, and musicians (pages 37–41). Help students play Conductor Concentration (pages 38 and 39) and make music stands (page 41).

Strings: The Violin Family

VIOLIN

The violin is one of four instruments in the string family. It is the smallest member of this family, but it makes the highest notes, giving it a soprano voice in an orchestra.

A violin is made from different types of wood, such as maple, spruce, pine, and ebony. Glue is the only thing used to hold together the parts of the violin.

The bow for a violin is often made from Brazilian Pernambuco wood and bleached hairs from a horse's tail.

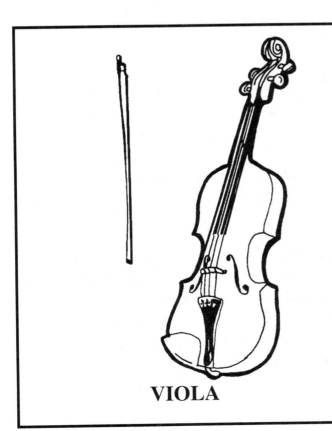

VIOLA

The viola is a little larger than the violin. Like the violin, it is made from different types of wood that are glued together. Even though the strings on a viola are longer and thicker than those on a violin, the two instruments are played in the same way.

A viola tends to sound less brilliant than a violin. It is often called the alto or tenor voice in an orchestra. Some composers use the viola when they wish to express gloom or sadness.

Strings: The Violin Family *(cont.)*

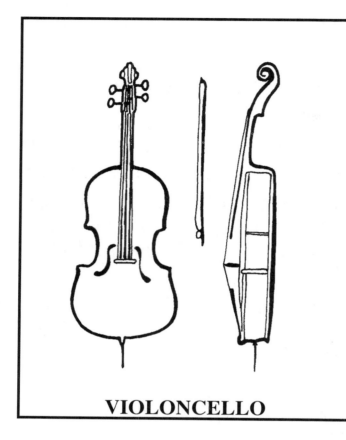

VIOLONCELLO

The violoncello is often called the cello. It is larger than both the violin or the viola. A peg is attached at the bottom of a violoncello so that it can be placed on the floor. The instrument then rests between the knees of the musician.

The violoncello can reach a greater range of notes than the viola. It can be used to play bass, tenor, and treble clefs. Composers use the violoncello to set the mood for many different kinds of music.

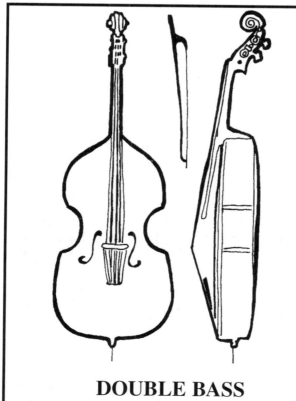

DOUBLE BASS

The double bass is sometimes called the string bass or contrabass. It measures over 6 feet (1.8 m) high, making it the largest member of the string family. It is called a bass voice in an orchestra because it makes the lowest notes of all the string instruments.

Like the violoncello, the double bass rests on the floor, using a peg placed at the bottom. The strings are thicker than other instruments in this family. The bow used for the double bass is shorter and heavier than other bows.

Make a Violin and Bow

Use the following directions to make a violin and bow.

Materials:

- empty tissue box
- 5 wide rubber bands
- rubber bands of different widths
- pencil, unsharpened

Directions:

1. Place a rubber band on your pencil by stretching it from the eraser to the other end.

2. Place four rubber bands on the tissue box over the opening. Be sure they are about ¹/₂ inch (1.25 cm) apart from one another.

3. Rub your bow (the pencil with the rubber band) across your violin (the tissue box with the rubber bands).

4. Now try using rubber bands of different widths.

How does the width of the rubber bands change the sound they make?

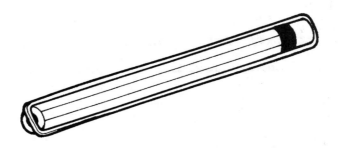

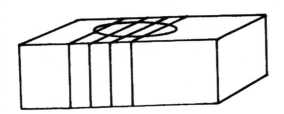
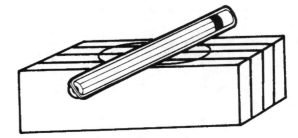

Woodwinds

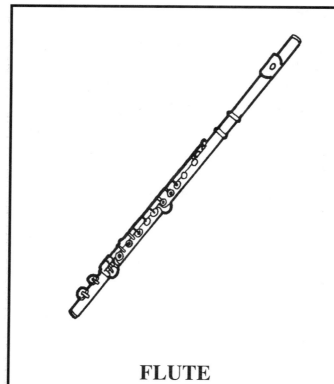

FLUTE

Most orchestras have three flute players. Long ago flutes were made from wood. Today flutes are made from three silver hollow tubes that fit together. The first tube has a hole for the musician to blow into. The other tubes have holes and keys for the musician's fingers.

The bottom keys on the flute have a hollow sound. The middle keys sound sweet and mellow. The upper keys provide a distinctly brilliant sound.

PICCOLO

The piccolo looks similar to a flute, but it is not even half as long. It has two sections that fit together. The piccolo plays notes that are higher than a flute. The piccolo's notes range from shrill to mellow and sweet.

Most musicians use wooden piccolos, although a few use metal ones. Almost all musicians who play piccolos also play the flute. As a result, some orchestras have one person who plays both the flute and the piccolo.

Woodwinds *(cont.)*

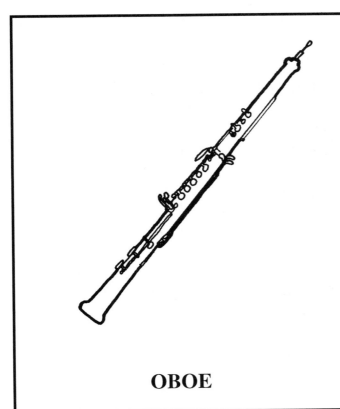

OBOE

The oboe is made from wood and has a double reed. It measures a little more than two feet (60 cm) long. It looks like a tube with a bell shape at the bottom. At the top of the oboe, there is a double reed mouthpiece surrounded by a small tube made from metal. The musician makes sound by gently blowing into the mouthpiece. There are holes along the tube that are opened and closed using keys. The keys control pitch.

The oboe plays the note A so that the other instruments in the orchestra can be tuned to it.

ENGLISH HORN

The name for the English horn does not seem to fit the instrument because it is not English and it is not really a horn. The English horn looks like the oboe, but it is a bit wider and measures about ten inches (25 cm) more in length. It is made from hard wood. Like the oboe, it has a double reed mouthpiece and a system of holes and keys along the tube. The tone of the English horn is much lower than that of the oboe.

Most orchestras have an oboe player who also plays the English horn.

Woodwinds *(cont.)*

CLARINET

Some clarinets are made from metal, although most are made from a type of wood called ebony. The clarinet looks like the oboe because it has a long tube with a bell shape at the end. It measures about two feet (60 cm) in length. At the top, there is a single reed mouthpiece.

Metal keys that cover holes along the tube control the pitch of the clarinet. The low notes sound pleasantly mellow. The middle notes sound sweetly distinct. The high notes make a shrill brilliant sound. In the woodwind family, the clarinet has the greatest range.

BASS CLARINET

The tube of a bass clarinet is twice as long as a regular clarinet. It has a long crook at the top and a turned up metal bell shape at the bottom. A peg in the bell shape allows the musician to rest the instrument on the floor. Like the clarinet, the bass clarinet has a single reed and metal keys. The notes played on a bass clarinet are lower than a regular clarinet and are often described as sounding sad.

Orchestras usually have three or four clarinet players. One of these musicians usually plays the bass clarinet when it is needed.

14

Woodwinds *(cont.)*

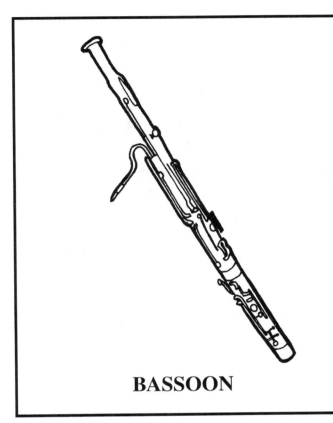

BASSOON

The bassoon is a long tube that measures about eight feet (2.4 m) in length. The tube is usually made from maple. Along the tube there are metal keys that are covered with nickel or silver. Toward the top of the instrument there is a double reed mouthpiece in a curved metal tube. The notes played on a bassoon have a low, mellow sound and often sound sad.

Most orchestras have three or four bassoon players. One of these musicians usually also plays the contrabassoon, or bass bassoon. Of the woodwind family, the contrabassoon plays the lowest notes.

SAXOPHONE

Saxophones are usually found in bands and sometimes in symphony orchestras. Saxophones, which are made from brass, come in different sizes. They can range from high C soprano saxophones to low bass saxophones. All saxophones have single reed mouthpieces. Saxophones are part of the woodwind instrument family because they have reeds.

Make a Flute

Use the following directions to make a flute.

Materials:

- yellow and black construction paper
- scissors
- tape
- glue

Directions:

1. Cut a rectangle from the yellow construction paper that is long and narrow.
2. Make a tube from the rectangle.
3. Use tape to keep the paper rolled into a tube.
4. Make the mouthpiece by cutting an oval from the black construction paper.
5. Glue the oval close to one end of the yellow tube.
6. Cut some small circles from the black construction paper.
7. Glue the black circles in a straight line along the yellow tube.

Now pretend to play your flute.

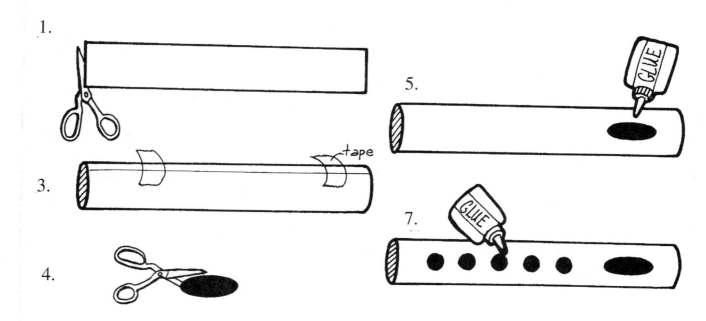

Brass

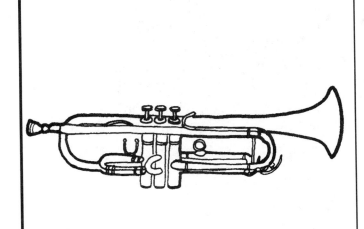

TRUMPET

The trumpet is a narrow tube made from brass. If the tube were unfolded and uncoiled, it would be about 8 feet (2.4 meters) long. At one end of the trumpet, there is a mouthpiece that looks like a shallow cup. At the other end, the tube widens and looks like a bell.

A musician plays the trumpet by blowing in the mouthpiece and pressing on three valves. The notes sound clear and distinct. However, the sound can be muted, or softened.

Most symphonies have three trumpet players.

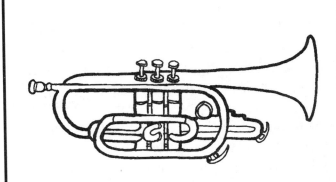

CORNET

The cornet, which is made from a brass tube and is played with valves, looks similar to the trumpet. However, the tube of a cornet is different from that of a trumpet because it is shaped more like a cone.

The notes of a cornet are mellow and full. It plays the highest notes in the brass family.

Orchestras do not use the cornet very often. However, it is a popular instrument among band musicians because it is easier to play than the trumpet.

Brass *(cont.)*

TROMBONE

The trombone is made from brass with one tube that fits inside of another tube. It does not have any valves or keys. A musician plays the trombone by blowing in the mouthpiece. The sound is changed by moving the tube that slides.

The music played on a trombone sounds full and deep. Most orchestras have one bass trombone and two tenor trombones. The tenor trombone is a little smaller than the bass trombone.

FLÜGELHORN

The flügelhorn looks like a cornet, but it is larger. It is made from brass and has a mouthpiece in the shape of a cup. The flügelhorn has three valves.

The musician must vibrate his or her lips and move the valves in order to play different notes on the flügelhorn. The sound from this instrument is described as rich and mellow. The flügelhorn is a popular instrument in jazz and concert bands.

18

Brass *(cont.)*

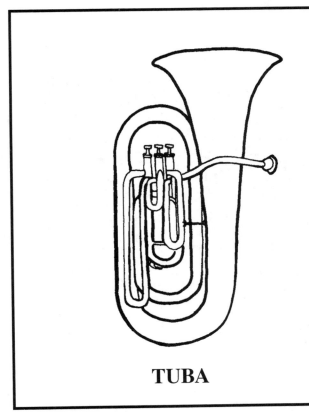

TUBA

The tuba is the largest brass instrument. It is used to play very deep notes. The tuba is made from a brass tube that is wrapped around in different directions.

A musician plays the tuba by blowing into a mouthpiece that is shaped like a cup and pressing on three valves. The sound comes out of a large bell shape that points upward.

Long ago tubas were used only in bands. However, today many symphony orchestras use upright tubas.

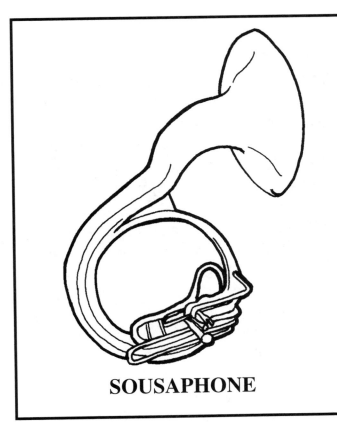

SOUSAPHONE

A sousaphone, or helicon, looks similar to a tuba. Like a tuba, it is a large brass instrument.

However, the tubing of a sousaphone is coiled in a circular shape so that the musician can wear it on his or her shoulder. The bell shape points upward, way above the musician's head. The bell can be taken off.

Since sousaphones are easier to carry than tubas, they are used in marching bands.

Brass *(cont.)*

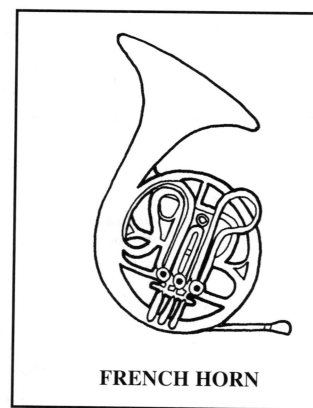

The French horn can be made from brass or nickel silver. It has a wide bell shape connected to 12-16 feet (3.6-4.8 m) of coiled tubing. The mouthpiece is shaped like a funnel. Most French horns have three or four valves. Some modern horns have a fifth valve that is used to mute the notes being played.

Music played on a French horn sounds smooth and mellow. Most orchestras have four or more French horns.

FRENCH HORN

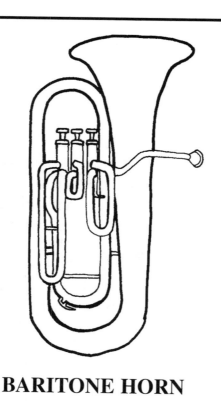

The baritone horn is like a tuba, only smaller and lighter. It is made from brass. At one end of the twisted tubing, there is a bell shape. At the other end, there is a cup-shaped mouthpiece. The musician plays the baritone horn by blowing into the mouthpiece and pressing on three valves. The notes played on a baritone horn sound lower than a tuba. The music sounds gentle and mellow.

The baritone horn is a popular band instrument.

BARITONE HORN

Make a Horn

Use the following directions to make a horn. Have an adult help you with the plastic tape.

Materials:

- 30 inches (70 cm) length of tubing
- funnel
- colored plastic tape
- unsharpened pencil
- stickers (optional)

Directions:

1. Use colored plastic tape or stickers to decorate the funnel.

2. Push one end of the tubing onto the narrow end of the funnel.

3. Use tape to hold the funnel and tubing together.

4. Make a mouthpiece by placing a piece of tape around the unused end of the tubing.

5. Make one loop in the tubing.

6. Place the pencil inside the loop where the tubing overlaps.

7. Use tape to hold the loop and pencil in place.

8. See if you can make different sounds with your horn. First, press your lips tightly together and blow through the mouthpiece. Then, slightly relax your lips and blow.

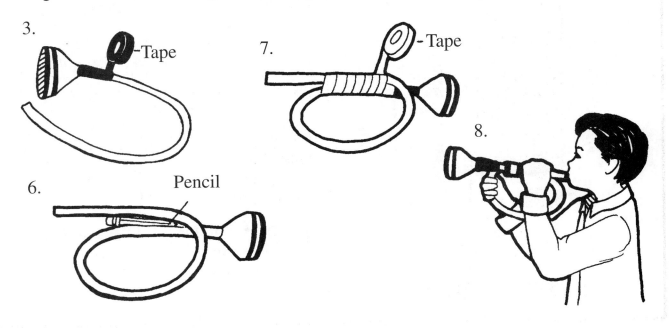

Percussion

KETTLEDRUM

The kettledrum is also called the timpani. This type of drum has a kettle made from copper or brass with calfskin or plastic tightly stretched over the top. Pedals and tuning screws are used to change the pitch. Different types of drumsticks can be used to change the tone. A sound from a kettledrum can be softened by placing a small piece of cloth on the drumhead.

Most symphony orchestras have two, three, or four kettledrums. These drums are very important instruments in orchestras.

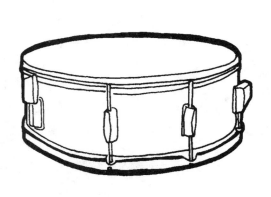

SNARE DRUM

The toy drums some children enjoy playing look very much like snare drums. A snare drum is shaped like a cylinder that is made from wood or brass. Calfskin or plastic is tightly stretched over the top and bottom of the cylinder. The side that the drummer beats is called the batter head. The other side is called the snare head. The snare head has strings that vibrate, making the drum sound like it rattles.

The snare drum is a very popular instrument in the orchestra and in many types of bands.

Percussion *(cont.)*

BASS DRUM

The bass drum is very large but looks like the snare drum. This drum is made from a cylinder of wood with a calfskin covering. The drumstick used to hit a bass drum is large and heavy. The head of the drumstick can be covered with wool or felt.

The bass drum has a low tone that can be played loudly or softly. It can be used in many different ways, such as to sound like thunderstorms, build excitement, or keep a marching beat. The bass drum is a popular instrument in orchestras, as well as marching bands.

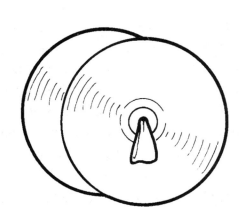

CYMBALS

Cymbals look like two large plates that have been hollowed out. There is a leather strap on the back of each cymbal. The musician places a leather strap on each hand to wear the cymbals. The musician can hit, touch, or scrape the cymbals together to play them.

Sometimes one cymbal will be hung up. Then the musician uses a mallet, or small hammer, to hit the cymbal. Using one cymbal, a cymbalist can make soft or loud sounds.

Percussion *(cont.)*

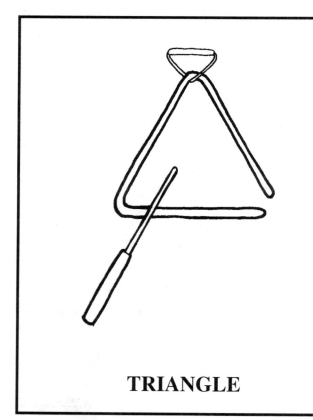

A steel bar is used to make a triangle. The ends of the bar do not touch each other, leaving a small opening in one corner. Triangles can measure from four to ten inches (10.5–25.5 cm), with the largest being the thickest. A short metal stick is used to hit the triangle.

At one time, most triangles were held by musicians. Today, they are usually hung on stands so musicians can use both of their hands to play these instruments.

TRIANGLE

Hardwood bars are used to make the keys of a xylophone. These bars are placed in the same order as the keys on a piano. Cords connect the bars to a frame. The bars are different sizes and lengths so the musician can play different notes. The musician plays the xylophone by hitting the bars with mallets or sticks.

XYLOPHONE

24

Percussion *(cont.)*

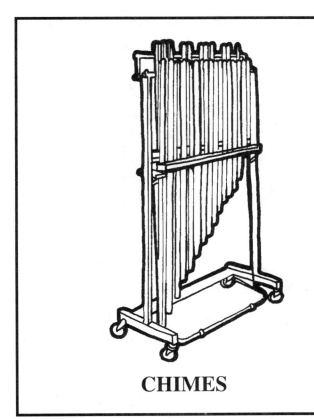

CHIMES

Chimes are pipes that are made from brass and covered with nickel. They are four to six feet (1.2 to 2 m) long with a diameter of about one inch (2.54 cm). A thick string is used to hang the pipes from a metal frame. There can be eight to thirteen pipes in a set of chimes. A mallet, or hammer, made from rawhide is used to hit close to the tops of the pipes. Chimes can be played so that they sound happy or sad.

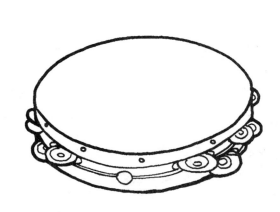

TAMBOURINE

The tambourine has a round frame that is made from wood and occasionally metal. The frame is usually 6–12 inches (15–30 cm) in diameter. Calfskin is tightly stretched over the frame. In the frame, there are several pairs of small disks made from metal. Wires are used to hold the disks in the frame. A musician can play a tambourine in many different ways, such as shaking it or using a hand, knee, or fingers to hit it. Sometimes a tambourine is played by connecting it to a stand and hitting it with a drumstick.

Make a Drum

Use the following directions to make a drum. Have an adult help you with the contact paper.

Materials:

- large can with a plastic lid
- contact paper
- crayons or markers
- scissors
- thick wooden ruler or wooden spoon

Directions:

1. Cut a piece of contact paper that will fit around the outside of the can.
2. Peel off the back of the contact paper and stick it onto the can.
3. Place the plastic lid on the can.
4. Use your wooden ruler or spoon to tap the top of the can.
5. Turn the can over, and use a ruler or spoon to tap the bottom of the can.
6. See how many different kinds of sounds you can make with your new drum.
7. Use the directions shown above to make some drums using cans that are different sizes. How does the sound change as the size of the drum changes?

Make a Xylophone

Use the following directions to make a xylophone. Have an adult help you.

Materials:

- eight fat pencils
- pencil sharpener
- scissors
- cardboard
- glue
- ruler
- wooden bead
- skewer

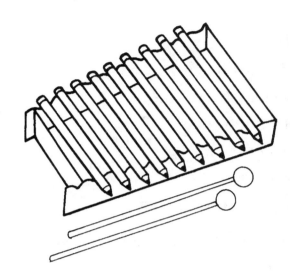

Directions:

1. Sharpen each pencil to a different length as shown here.

2. Use a cardboard frame that looks like the one below. Use these measurements to make the frame.

sides:	8.5 inches (21 cm) long
long end:	6 inches (15 cm) long
short end:	4.5 inches (11 cm) long

3. Glue the pieces of the frame together.

4. Place the pencils on the frame as shown below.

5. Make a beater by gluing a wooden bead onto a skewer.

6. Now play your xylophone.

2.

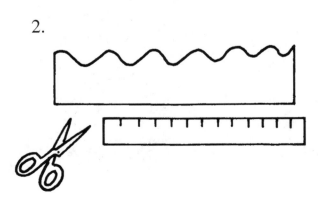

4.

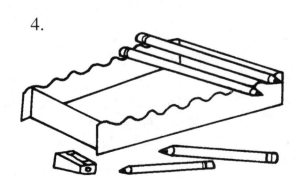

Make a Tambourine

Use the following directions to make a tambourine. Have an adult help you use the stapler.

Materials:

- dried beans (seeds may be substituted)
- two disposable pie tins
- stapler
- tempera paint
- paintbrushes
- streamers or ribbon (optional)

Directions:

1. Paint decorations on the outside of each pie tin. Allow the paint to dry.

2. Place some dried beans in one pie tin.

3. Place the other pie tin upside down on top of the tin with the dried beans.

4. Carefully staple along the rims to join the two pie tins together.

5. You may wish to staple streamers or pieces of ribbon onto your tambourine.

6. Hold your tambourine with one hand and tap it against the palm of your other hand. Try playing your tambourine along with some music.

Make Cymbals

Cymbals

Have an adult help you make some cymbals using the following directions.

Materials:

- pen or sharpened pencil
- two cabinet knobs
- two disposable pie tins

Directions:

1. Use the point of a pen or pencil to poke a small hole in the middle of each pie tin.

2. Attach the cabinet knobs to the pie tins by screwing them into the holes.

3. Hold each pie tin by the cabinet knob. Then clap the pie tins together.

Finger Cymbals

Now make some cymbals that are small enough to fit on your fingers.

Materials:

- hammer
- small nail
- two metal bottle caps
- yarn or string

Directions:

1. Have an adult use a hammer and nail to make two small holes in the center of each bottle cap.

2. Loop a small piece of yarn through the holes in each bottle cap. Then tie a knot in each piece of yarn.

3. Slip your fingers into the loops. Pinch your fingers together to play your cymbals.

Other Popular Instruments

GUITAR

The guitar is a stringed instrument. However, it does not belong to the string family because it is not played with a bow. The body of the guitar is shaped like a violin with a large flat back and a sound hole in the front. The neck is long and has ridges on it.

The classical, or Spanish, guitar is light and easy to carry. It has six strings that are usually made from nylon. The strings are tied to tuning pegs at the end of the neck. Notes are played by plucking or strumming the strings.

Many types of guitars, including classical, folk, steel-strung acoustic, and electric are all popular today.

BANJO

The banjo is a stringed instrument. However, like the guitar, it is not part of the string family because it is not played with a bow. It is about the size of a guitar. Its body is large, round, and hollow. The banjo does not have a sound hole. Its neck is very long and has ridges on it. It has four strings that are tied to tuning pegs at the end of the neck. Notes are played by plucking the strings.

Banjos are frequently used in jazz bands and music halls.

Other Popular Instruments *(cont.)*

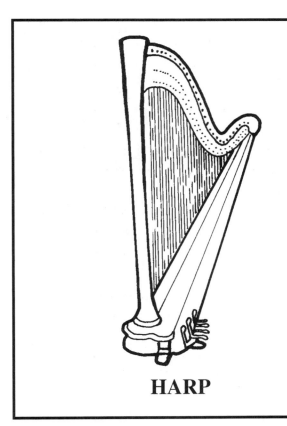

HARP

The harp is the largest instrument in an orchestra. It is four feet (1.2 m) wide and five feet (1.5 m) tall. This instrument is played using forty-seven different colored strings and seven pedals. Wire is used for the longest strings. The other strings are usually made from nylon. The musician uses six fingers and both thumbs to pluck the strings. The little fingers are not used. The pedals are used to play music in different keys. The musician must use both feet on these pedals.

Most orchestras have one harp, although some have two harps.

PIANO

A piano is a keyboard instrument. It is in the percussion family because inside it has wooden hammers, with tips covered by felt, that strike strings made from steel. The hammers are controlled by the keyboard. The keyboard has 88 keys. The white keys are made from ivory or plastic. The black keys are made from ebony or plastic. A piano can have two or three pedals. The pedals are used to make the notes being played sound louder or softer.

Modern pianos are divided into two groups based on their shapes: grand and upright.

Harp Directions

Make a harp using the directions shown below and the pattern shown on page 33. Have an adult help you with this activity.

Materials:

- harp pattern (page 33)
- piece of heavy cardboard
- pencil
- scissors
- yarn

Directions:

1. Trace the harp pattern onto a piece of heavy cardboard.

2. Cut out the pattern from the cardboard.

3. Use a sharp pencil point to make eight holes along the inside, curved edge at the top and the inside, slanted edge of the cardboard pattern. Be sure the holes are about the same distance apart.

4. Cut a long piece of yarn. Tie a knot in one end. Slip the other end through the first hole at the top.

5. String the yarn through the first hole at the bottom. Then pull it across to the second hole at the bottom and string it through.

6. String the yarn through the second hole at the top. Then pull it across to the third hole at the top and string it through.

7. Continue stringing the yarn through the rest of the holes. After stringing all of the holes, tie a knot in the yarn next to the last hole, and cut off any extra yarn.

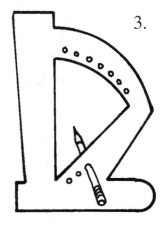 3.

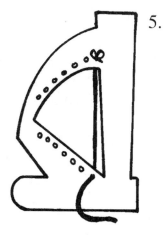 5.

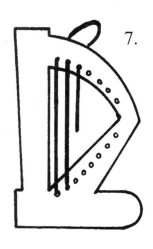 7.

Harp Pattern

Make a harp using the directions on page 32 and the pattern shown below.

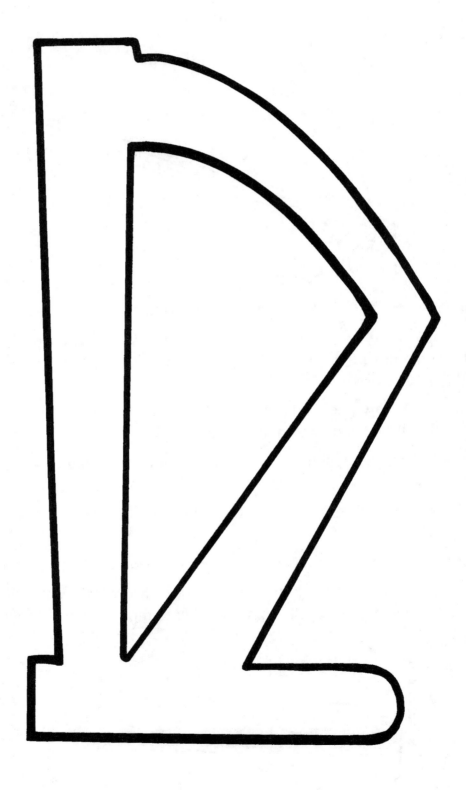

Make a Banjo

Use the following directions to make a banjo. Be sure to ask an adult to help you.

Materials:

- round cardboard container
- scissors
- ruler
- six thumb tacks
- nylon fishing line
- white tempera paint
- paintbrushes
- glue

Directions:

1. Have an adult cut a slit in each side of the container.

2. Take the top off the container. Put glue on the slits and gently push the ruler through them. Have the ruler stick out of the other end by about 1 inch (2.5 cm). Allow the glue to dry.

3. Have an adult help you cut an arc in the top of the container as shown below. Pull the arc so that it bends up and make four small cuts in it.

4. Glue the top onto the container. Allow the glue to dry. Paint the top white. Allow the paint to dry.

5. Carefully place two thumb tacks in the end of the ruler that is closest to the container.

6. Carefully place two thumb tacks on the sides of the ruler at the other end.

7. Tie the fishing line from the bottom thumb tack through the arc to the thumb tack on the side of the neck. Do the same with three more pieces of fishing line.

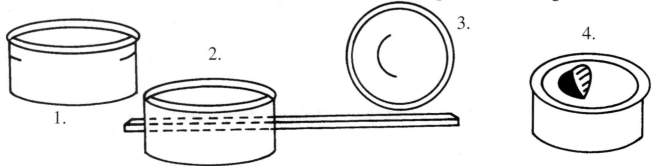

Your Favorite Instrument

Which instrument do you like best? Use the space below to draw a picture of yourself playing that instrument.

Symphony Orchestra Seating

The following diagram shows one possible seating arrangement for a symphony orchestra. You may wish to create a bulletin board using this diagram and the pictures of different instruments (pages 9–31) and/or make an overhead transparency of this page to use when presenting this information to the class.

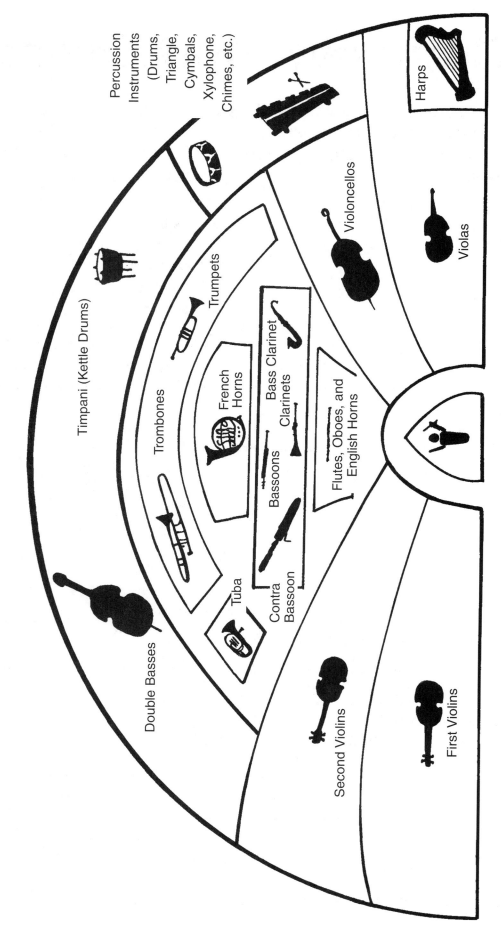

Percussion Instruments (Drums, Triangle, Cymbals, Xylophone, Chimes, etc.)

Harps

Violoncellos

Violas

Trumpets

Timpani (Kettle Drums)

Trombones

French Horns

Bass Clarinet

Clarinets

Bassoons

Flutes, Oboes, and English Horns

Contra Bassoon

Tuba

Double Basses

Second Violins

First Violins

Composer and Conductor

A composer is a person who writes music. A conductor is a person who leads the symphony orchestra when the music is played. Color the finger puppets shown below. Glue them onto tagboard. Cut them out. Then play with the puppets.

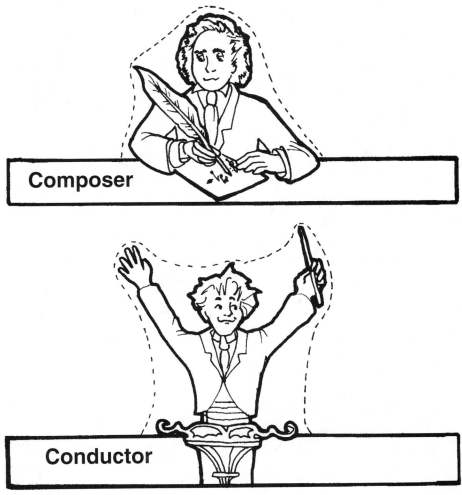

Composer

Conductor

You can learn the names of the notes. Use the saying "Every Good Boy Does Fine," to remember the notes on the lines are E, G, B, D, F. Use the word "FACE" to remember the notes in the spaces are F, A, C, E.

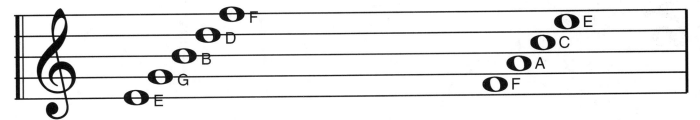

Now play Concentration using the Conductor Cards (pages 38-39).

Conductor Cards

Introduce some famous conductors, using the cards shown below and on page 39. Then reproduce twice and cut apart the cards so that each student has two sets. Show students how to play Concentration by matching the pictures of the conductors.

Sir George Solti

Leonard Bernstein

Herbert von Karajan

Arturo Toscanini

Conductor Cards *(cont.)*

Have students use the cards shown below and on page 38 to play Concentration.

Leopold Stokowski

Sir Thomas Beecham

John Williams

Andre Previn

Musician

A musician is a person who plays music. Here is a poem about being a musician. You may wish to use some of the instruments you made as you read aloud the poem. Make a music stand using the directions on page 41. You can use this when you pretend to be a musician.

I Am a Fine Musician
(Traditional)

I am a fine musician, I travel round the world.
    (Clap hands.)
I can play my violin, my violin, my violin.
    (Pretend to play a violin.)
I can play my violin, fiddle-dee-dee-da.

I am a fine musician, I travel round the world.
    (Clap hands.)
I can blow my trumpet, my trumpet, my trumpet.
    (Pretend to blow a trumpet.)
I can blow my trumpet, toot-toot-toot-toot-toot.

I am a fine musician, I travel round the world.
    (Clap hands.)
I can crash my cymbals, my cymbals, my cymbals.
    (Pretend to crash some cymbals.)
I can crash my cymbals, crash-crash-crash-crash-bang.

I am a fine musician, I travel round the world.
    (Clap hands.)
I can beat my big loud drum, big loud drum, big loud drum.
    (Pretend to beat the drum.)
I can beat my big loud drum, boom-boom-boom-boom-boom.

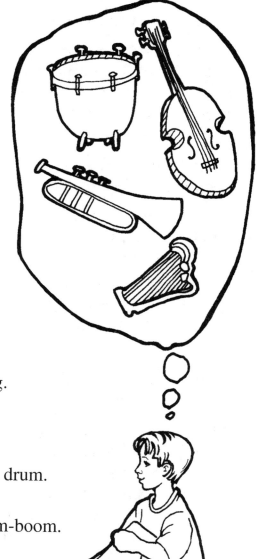

40

Music Stand

Make one or more music stands for students to use when role-playing how to be a musician.

Materials: thick cardboard, thin cardboard, ruler, pencil, scissors, glue, masking tape, cardboard tubes (long), coffee can, plaster of Paris, spoon

Directions:

1. Draw and cut out a rectangle on the thin cardboard that is 33 x 18 inches (84 x 46 cm).

2. Divide the rectangle into four sections:

   Section A = 12 x 18 inches (30 x 46 cm),
   Section B = 12 x 18 inches (30 x 46 cm),
   Section C = 6 x 18 inches (15 x 46 cm),
   Section D = 3 x 18 inches (8 x 46 cm).

3. Make a triangle that can stand up by folding on the lines between sections. Then glue Section A to Section D. Allow the glue to dry.

4. Draw and cut out a rectangle on the thick cardboard that is 8 x 18 inches (20 x 46 cm).

5. Glue the rectangle under Section C of the triangle. Three edges of the thick cardboard should be flush with Section C. The fourth edge should stick out beyond Section B.

6. Use masking tape to connect several cardboard tubes together.

7. Mix the plaster of Paris according to the directions on the package. Pour plaster into the coffee can until it is half full. Place one end of the tubes into the plaster. Be sure the tubes are standing straight and are in the center of the plaster. Allow the plaster to harden.

8. Use masking tape to connect the other end of the tubes to Section A.

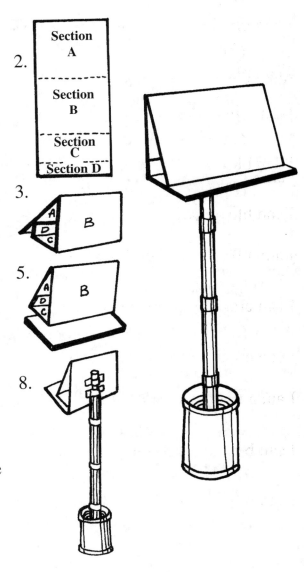

Sample Plans

Day 1: Show students the picture of composer Sergei Prokofiev (page 45) and read the biographical sketch. Use a globe or world map to point out where Ukraine is in relationship to your community. Read aloud "The Story of Peter and the Wolf" (pages 49 and 50). Discuss the story and play the recording of *Peter and the Wolf.* Display the flannel board pieces (pages 46 and 47) as characters are introduced.

Day 2: Review the instruments used for the different characters in the story: the strings (pages 9 and 10) play Peter's song, the flute (page 12) represents the bird, the oboe (page 13) the duck, the clarinet (page 14) the cat, the bassoon (page 15) Peter's grandfather, the French horn (page 20) the wolf, and the kettledrum and bass drum (pages 22 and 23) the hunters.

Show the pictures of the string instruments (violin, viola, violoncello, double bass). Point out how the instruments differ in size and, therefore, make different sounds. Call students' attention to the strings on each instrument. Ask volunteers to count the number of strings. Do the same for the black knobs that are located at the top of the instruments. Explain that these black knobs wind the strings so that they can be used to play certain notes. Then show students the chin rests located at the bottoms of the violin and the viola where the musician puts her/his chin when playing. Tell students that a bow is moved across the strings to play the violin, viola, violoncello, and double bass. To play the correct notes of music, the musician must place her/his fingers in special places on the strings. Play the recording of *Peter and the Wolf* and have students listen for the string instruments. Ask students to raise the pictures of the string instruments every time they are heard.

Show the pictures of the woodwinds (flute, oboe, clarinet, and bassoon). Explain that these are called woodwinds because musicians have to blow into the mouthpieces that have single or double reeds. If possible, show students a reed. Point out that woodwinds vary in size and produce different sounds. Call students' attention to the valves on the woodwinds. Tell students that every time a different valve is pressed down, a different sound is heard. Invite volunteers to count the number of valves. Show the picture of the brass instrument (French horn). Call students' attention to the valves. Invite a volunteer to count the number of valves. Play the recording of *Peter and the Wolf* a second time and have students listen for the woodwind and brass instruments. Ask students to raise the pictures of the woodwind and brass instruments every time they are heard. Model which cards to raise to help students know when each instrument is being played.

Show the pictures of the percussion instruments (kettledrum and bass drum). Explain that these instruments are played with a mallet. The bass drum is deeper in sound because of its size. Play the recording of *Peter and the Wolf* a third time and have students listen for the percussion instruments. Ask students to raise the pictures of the drums every time they are heard.

Sample Plans (cont.)

Day 3: Read aloud a book that tells the story of *Peter and the Wolf.* (See the bibliography, page 144). Allow students to match the flannel board pieces of the characters (pages 46-47) with the pictures of the instruments that represent those characters: the strings for Peter, the flute for the bird, the oboe for the duck, the clarinet for the cat, the bassoon for Peter's grandfather, the French horn for the wolf, and the kettledrum and bass drum for the hunters. Have students compare and contrast the different instruments. Examples: *A violin and a double bass are string instruments. A violin is smaller than a double bass.* Help students use the correct names for the instruments.

Reproduce the little book (pages 51–55) for students. Read the little books together. Review in the little book the instruments that are used to represent the different characters. Then invite students to role-play the story.

Play the recording of *Peter and the Wolf.* Encourage students to use their little books to follow along with the story. Have students make a wolf shadow puppet (page 48). Turn out the classroom lights and turn on an overhead projector or a lamp without a shade. Invite students to take turns holding their puppets in front of the bright light so that they project shadows onto a screen or blank wall. Have the students pretend to be the wolf and retell the story. You may wish to have individual students retell the story or have the class participate in a group retelling. Stress the importance of telling the story events in the correct order.

Review the jobs of the musicians (page 40). Have students pretend to be the musicians playing *Peter and the Wolf.* As they listen to the recording again, allow them to pretend to play their violins, flutes, horns, and drums.

Day 4: If you have a metronome, show students how it can be used to mark the timing of different beats. Help students learn how to clap to the beat of poems or nursery rhymes. Then play the recording of *Peter and the Wolf.* Call students' attention to the timing of the music. Show them how to clap to the beat of the music.

Review the job of a conductor (pages 37–39). Demonstrate how a conductor might move a baton. Remind students about safety rules so they will not touch each other during this activity. Then play the recording again and have them pretend to be conductors using unsharpened pencils or rulers as batons. Point out to students that they must move their batons to the beat of the music.

Provide drawing materials. Ask students to draw or paint pictures of their favorite parts of the story. Play the recording of *Peter and the Wolf* while students are participating in this art activity. Display these pictures.

Sample Plans *(cont.)*

Day 5: Play the recording of *Peter and the Wolf.* Ask students to name the animals that are characters in the story. Teach students the following finger play.

Little Bird
(Author Unknown)

I saw a little bird go hop, hop, hop.
(Place the tips of the first two fingers on the thumb and move the wrist to make a hopping motion.)
I told the little bird to stop, stop, stop.
(Point and shake the index finger each time you say the word stop.)
I went to the window to say, "How do you do?"
(Place hand out as if to shake hands with another person.)
It wagged its little tail
(Hold hand with fingers up and shake them back and forth.)
And away it flew.
(Wiggle fingers and raise hands over head.)

Then reproduce and make an overhead transparency of the poems (page 56). Read the poems together. Call students' attention to the rhyming words. You may wish to have students circle or underline the rhyming words on their copies of the poems.

Make an overhead transparency or a chart on the chalkboard for Rhyming Words (page 57). Ask students to brainstorm a list of words that rhyme with *nest, duck, cat,* and *tail.* Write students' suggestions on the transparency or chalkboard. Discuss the differences in meanings for the homonyms *pale* and *pail, sale* and *sail,* as well as *tail* and *tale.*

Display books, magazines, and pictures of birds, ducks, cats, and wolves. Learn more about these animals. Further discussion or investigation may include the different types of each species, physical descriptions, habitats, sources of food, adaptations to their environments, and enemies.

You may wish to explain to students that many people thought that wolves were dangerous animals and believed that they should all be killed. As a result the wolf population was drastically reduced. Point out that some people's attitudes towards wolves have changed. Tell students that wolves are being reintroduced into some wilderness areas.

Have students tell facts that they have learned about the different animals. Ask volunteers to display the appropriate flannel board pieces (pages 46 and 47) as students tell some facts that they have learned about birds, ducks, cats, and wolves.

44

About the Composer

Sergei Prokofiev was born in Sontsovka, Ukraine, in 1891. People could tell that Prokofiev was musically gifted at an early age. He wrote his first opera when he was only twelve years old. He went to school at the St. Petersburg Conservatory where he became an excellent pianist and composer. A revolution began in the former Soviet Union in 1917, so Prokofiev moved to Paris, France. He returned to his homeland in 1932. When he returned, Prokofiev was celebrated as a hero and musical wonder. He wrote operas, concertos, symphonies, music for films, scores for ballets, as well as *Peter and the Wolf,* a popular composition for children.

Prokofiev died in Moscow in 1953. Today his music is very popular, and it is frequently played by symphony orchestras.

Flannel Board Patterns

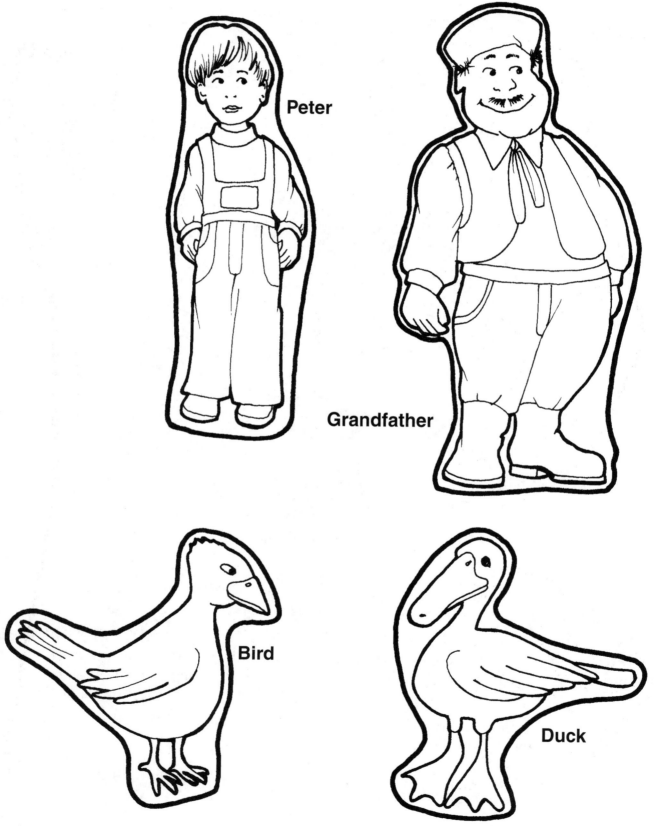

Peter

Grandfather

Bird

Duck

46

Flannel Board Patterns *(cont.)*

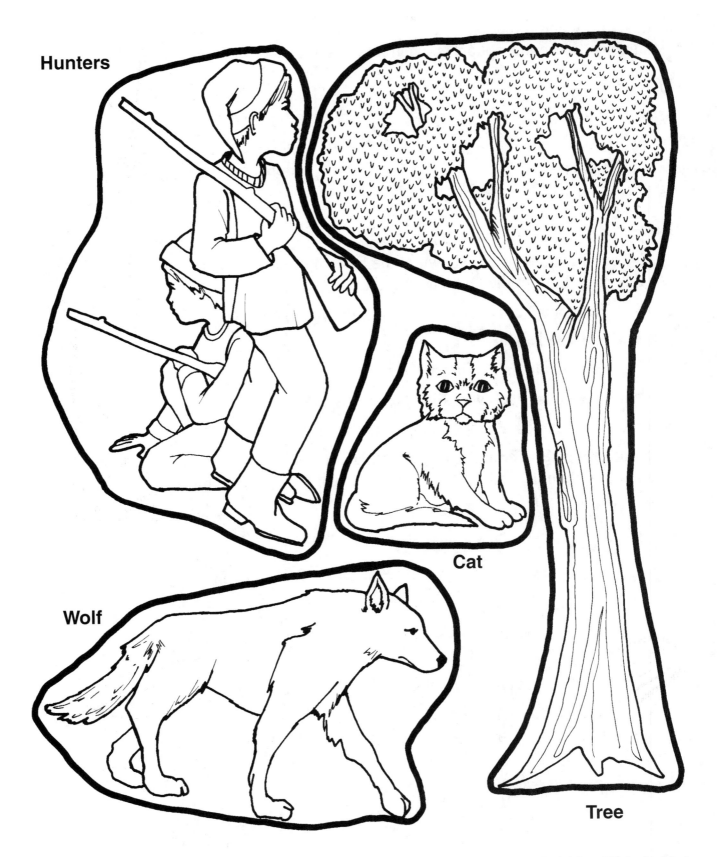

Hunters

Cat

Wolf

Tree

Wolf Shadow Puppet

Use the pattern and directions shown below to help students make a wolf shadow puppet. Ask students to use their puppets when retelling the story of *Peter and the Wolf*.

Materials:

- wolf pattern
- tagboard
- masking tape
- hole puncher

- ruler or tape measure
- wire coat hanger
- wire cutters
- scissors

Directions:

1. Cut out the wolf pattern shown at the bottom of the page and trace onto a piece of tagboard. Cut out the tagboard patterns.

2. Use a hole puncher to make holes for the eyes on the tagboard patterns.

3. Straighten the hangers.

4. Use the wire cutters to cut off 11 inches (28 cm) of wire from each hanger.

5. Bend one end of each wire to make an L shape.

6. Tape the L-shaped end of each wire to the back of a tagboard wolf.

7. Turn off the classroom lights and hold a puppet in front of an overhead projector or a lamp without a shade. Use a screen or blank wall to see the shadow from the puppet.

The Story of Peter and the Wolf

Peter opened the gate and went into the meadow. *(Listen for violins, violas, cellos, and bass violins.)*

The bird flew up to a branch on the tree and chirped, "All is quiet." *(Listen for the flute.)*

The duck came along. It went through the gate to take a swim in the pond. *(Listen for the oboe.)*

The bird flew to the duck and asked, "What kind of a bird are you, if you can't fly?"

The duck replied, "What kind of a bird are you, if you can't swim?"

Peter saw the cat crawling through the grass. *(Listen for the clarinet.)*

The cat thought this would be a good time to catch the bird. But Peter yelled to the bird, and it quickly flew into the tree. The duck swam in the middle of the pond and quacked angrily at the cat.

Grandfather walked out into the meadow. *(Listen for the bassoon.)*

Grandfather was angry to find the gate had been left wide open. He scolded Peter and asked, "If a wolf came out of the forest what would you do then?"

Peter thought, "I'm not afraid of wolves."

Grandfather took Peter's hand, locked the gate, and took him back home. Just then a big gray wolf came out of the forest. *(Listen for the French horn.)*

When the cat saw the wolf, it climbed up into a tree. The duck was in the middle of the pond. It quacked with such excitement that it jumped out of the pond. The wolf caught the duck and swallowed it in one gulp.

The Story of Peter and the Wolf *(cont.)*

The cat was sitting on one branch of the tree. The bird was on another branch, being careful not to get too close to the cat. All the while the wolf walked around and around the tree.

Peter stood behind the locked gate and watched everything. Then he ran home. Soon he returned with a strong rope. Peter threw the rope over a branch of the tree. Then he tied the rope and climbed up it. He told the bird to fly down close to the wolf's head. The wolf tried and tried to catch the little bird but could not.

In the meantime, Peter made a lasso out of the rope. He lowered it and caught the wolf's tail.

The wolf could not get loose. Peter tied the other end of the rope to the tree. When the wolf tried to get free, the rope got tighter on its tail.

Suddenly hunters came out of the forest, shooting at the wolf. *(Listen for the kettledrum and bass drum.)*

Peter shouted, "Don't shoot. The bird and I have caught the wolf. Help us take it to the zoo."

Imagine the happy march to the zoo. Peter was at the head of the line. Then came the hunters bringing the wolf.

Then came Grandfather who said, "What if Peter had not caught the wolf? It was a dangerous thing to do."

The bird flew about cheerfully chirping, "What brave fellows Peter and I were. Look what we have caught."

(If you listen very carefully, you will hear the duck quacking. The wolf was in such a hurry it swallowed the duck alive.)

Making Little Books

PETER AND THE WOLF

Name _____

viola

violoncello

double bass

Peter went into the meadow.

1

51

Making Little Books *(cont.)*

flute

A little bird sat on a tree branch.

2

oboe

Then a duck came.

3

52

Making Little Books *(cont.)*

clarinet

A cat was in the grass.

4

bassoon

Grandpa came out of the house.

5

Making Little Books *(cont.)*

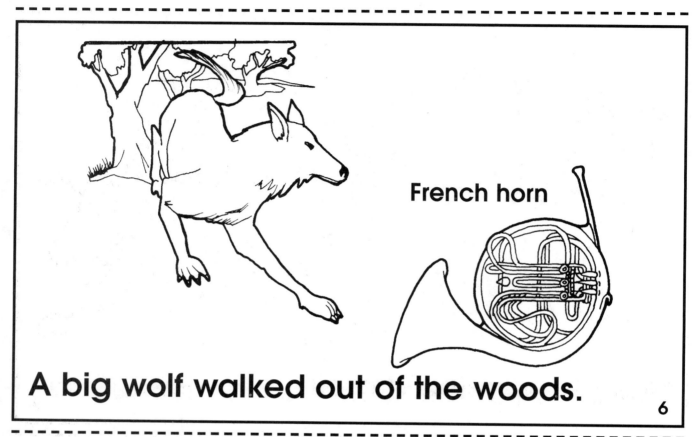

French horn

A big wolf walked out of the woods.

6

kettledrum

bass drum

The hunters came out of the forest.

7

Making Little Books (cont.)

There was a triumphant procession.

8

The little bird sang, "Peter and I are very smart!"

9

Poems

Fly, little birdie.
Fly up to the sky.
Tell me, sweet birdie,
Who taught you to fly?

A duck can dive,
And he can swim.
But when he walks,
I laugh at him.

I know a little cat
Who loves to purr and play,
Then curls up on a mat
And sleeps the day away.

Little gray wolf,
This is the way
You learn to hunt
And catch your prey.

Rhyming Words

Write rhyming words for the word at the top of each box. The first one has been done for you.

nest

1. best
2. _____
3. _____
4. _____
5. _____

duck

1. _____
2. _____
3. _____
4. _____
5. _____

cat

1. _____
2. _____
3. _____
4. _____
5. _____

tail

1. _____
2. _____
3. _____
4. _____
5. _____

Tangrams

Cut along the lines to make your own set of tangram pieces. Use the tangram pieces to make a wolf, duck, and cat. The pictures shown on this page will help you get started.

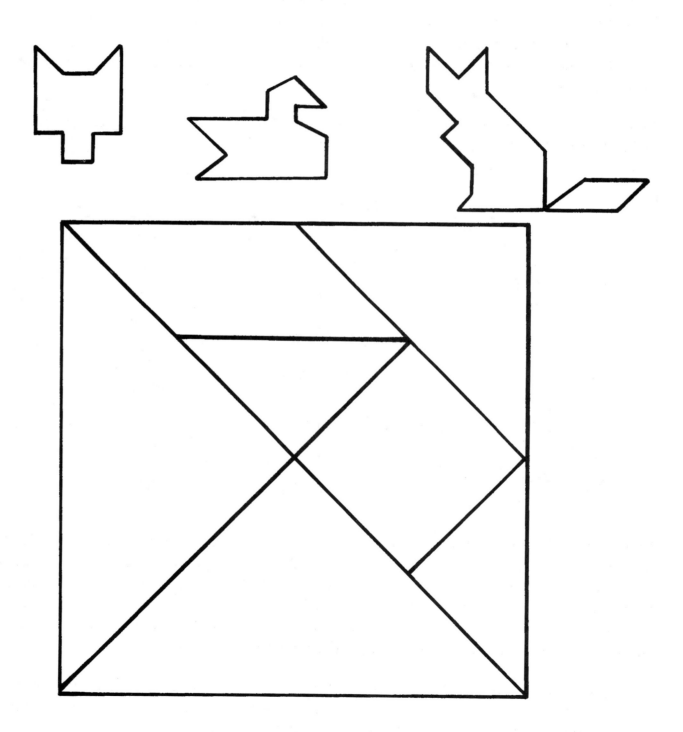

58

Sample Plans—*Surprise Symphony*

Day 1: Show students the picture of the composer, Franz Joseph Haydn (page 62), and read aloud the biographical sketch. Use a globe or world map to point out where Austria is in relationship to your community. Ask students if they know what a symphony is. Lead them to conclude that a symphony is a piece of music written by a composer that is played by musicians in an orchestra. Review the jobs that composers, conductors, and musicians do.

Write the word *surprise* on the chalkboard. Ask students to tell about a time when they were *surprised*. Create an idea web with *surprise* in the center circle and students' responses in surrounding circles.

Sample Idea Web

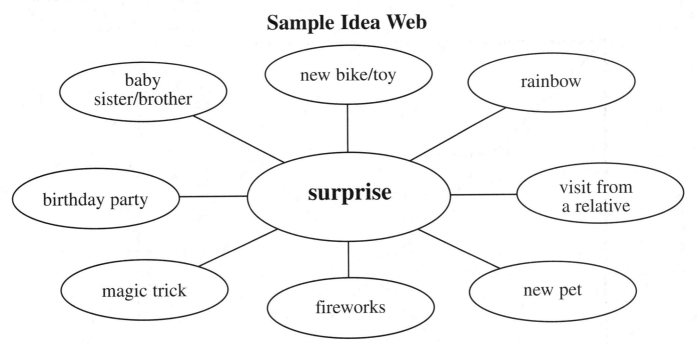

Read aloud "The Story of the Surprise Symphony" (page 64). Discuss the story. Then play the recording of the *Surprise Symphony*. Display the flannel board pieces (page 63) to tell the story as the music is being played. Ask students to name the surprise that they hear in the symphony. Point out how the music becomes softer and then the loud chord is heard. Explain that this is the surprise. Take a poll to see how many students were surprised by the loud chord. Have students help you count as you take the poll.

Day 2: Play the recording of the *Surprise Symphony*. Ask students to name instruments that they hear during the symphony. You may wish to have students raise the pictures of the instrument cards as they hear the different instruments.

Sample Plans—*Surprise Symphony* (cont.)

Day 3: Review the events that took place in "The Story of the *Surprise Symphony*" (page 64). Write the sequence of events on the chalkboard or an overhead transparency. Call students' attention to the order of the events. Play the recording of the *Surprise Symphony*. Have students role-play the events of the story. Students' role-playing should include pretending to eat dinner, falling asleep while listening to the music, and jumping awake when the loud chord is heard.

Ask volunteers to retell "The Story of the *Surprise Symphony*." You may wish to have students use the composer finger puppet (page 37) and pretend to be Haydn when retelling the story. Encourage students to put the story events in the correct order. Invite volunteers to use the flannel pieces as they retell the story.

Replay the recording of the *Surprise Symphony*. Have some students pretend to be musicians playing the music. Invite them to use the music stand (page 41) as they role-play being musicians. Have other students pretend to be conductors. Ask them to pretend they are leading the orchestra as the music is played.

Day 4: Distribute drawing paper to students. Help students fold their papers in half. As they listen to the recording of the *Surprise Symphony,* ask them to do the following art activity. Have them draw the face of a sleeping person on one side of their papers. Then, have them draw the face of a surprised person on the other side of their papers. Invite students to share their pictures with the class, or display them in the classroom.

Reproduce the little book (pages 65 and 66) for students. Allow students to color the pictures in the books. Read the little books together. Ask volunteers to retell the story using their little books.

Replay the recording of the *Surprise Symphony*. Have students follow along in their little books as they listen to the music. Encourage students to take home their little books and share them with family members.

Sample Plans—*Surprise Symphony* (cont.)

Day 5: Write the words *softer* and *louder* on the chalkboard. Discuss the meanings of these words. Help students discriminate between left and right. Then play the recording and have students raise their right hands if the music becomes softer and their left hands if the music becomes louder.

Invite students to participate in one or more of the following activities:

- Have students make toy drums, using the directions on page 26. Start the recording of the *Surprise Symphony*. When the loud chord is played, have students beat their drums.

- Give each student a toy instrument. Have the students play their toy instruments more and more quietly. Then have them play the instruments very loudly.

- Have students use the song BINGO to practice singing increasingly softer until they are only mouthing the words. Then have them sing the words as loudly as they can without shouting.

- Distribute crayons and drawing paper to students. Play the recording of the *Surprise Symphony*. Tell students to listen carefully to the music. Encourage students to let the music guide them as they draw their pictures. Tell them to draw what the music makes them think of.

- Have students stand in a circle. Play the recording. As the music gets softer, have students crouch. When the loud chord is heard, have students jump.

- Help students make puppets out of socks. Play the recording. Have students use their puppets to show the events of the story. Students' puppets should show how the audience fell asleep while listening to the music. Then, the puppets should show how the audience was suddenly awakened when the surprise chord was played.

- Demonstrate how a conductor might move a baton. Remind students about safety rules so they will not touch each other during this activity. Then play the recording. Have students pretend to be conductors, using unsharpened pencils or rulers as batons. Point out to students that they must move their batons to the beat of the music.

- Explain to students that Haydn was friends with another famous composer by the name of Wolfgang Amadeus Mozart. Discuss what friendship means. You may wish to create an idea web for the word *friendship*.

About the Composer

Franz Joseph Haydn was born in Austria in 1732. When he was young, he went to a choir school in Vienna. The school provided him with an excellent background in music. He wrote his first symphonies when he was 27 years old. During his lifetime, he wrote a total of 104 symphonies. As a result, many people think of Haydn as one of the main creators of the symphony. However, Haydn wrote much more than just symphonies. He also wrote chamber music, string quartets, string and piano trios, concertos, sonatas, and operas, in addition to other types of music.

Haydn was loved and respected during his lifetime. Many affectionately refer to him as "Papa Haydn." Today his music continues to be popular and is frequently played on classical radio stations.

Flannel Board Patterns

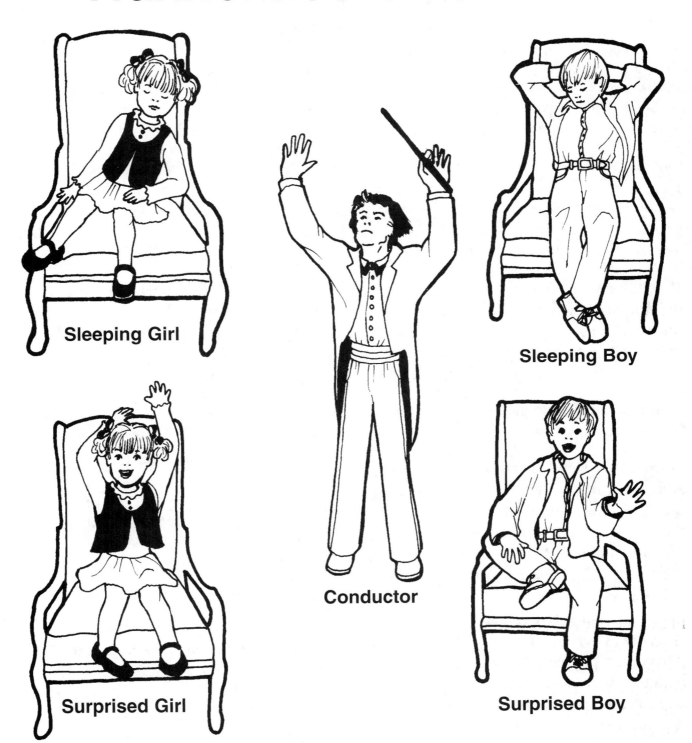

Sleeping Girl

Conductor

Sleeping Boy

Surprised Girl

Surprised Boy

The Story of the *Surprise Symphony*

Franz Joseph Haydn was a composer who loved to write music. Since Haydn was a musician, he enjoyed playing his music at "dinner concerts." These concerts were special because they took place after the audience, or listeners, had eaten dinner.

One night Haydn decided to conduct a new piece of music that he had composed. He picked up his baton, stood in front of the orchestra, and gave the signal for the musicians to begin playing the music. As the music was being played, Haydn looked around at the people who were supposed to be listening. He was sad to discover that they were falling asleep. He wondered what he could do about this problem.

Haydn knew that the people felt relaxed after eating the delicious dinner. However, he did not want them to fall asleep while his music was being played. He decided that he must try to do something to make sure the people stayed awake. That night he went home and composed a new symphony. He was very proud of this composition because it had a surprise that would keep the people awake at the next dinner concert.

At the next dinner concert, Haydn could hardly wait to see what the people thought of his new composition. He wondered what they would do when they heard his surprise.

Once again, Haydn picked up his baton. He stood in front of the orchestra and gave them the signal to begin playing the music. When the music started, Hadyn looked around to see what the people were doing. As usual they were falling asleep. Haydn thought, "Now it's time for my surprise." The music got softer and softer. Suddenly there was a very loud chord. When the loud chord was played, the people were surprised. They sat straight up in their seats. From that day forward, the people never again fell asleep while listening to Haydn's music. Haydn was happy that his music had been so successful. He decided to call his new symphony the *Surprise Symphony*.

64

Making Little Books

The Surprise Symphony

Name _____

The people came to hear Franz Joseph Haydn perform at a dinner concert. First, the people ate a delicious dinner.

2

Making Little Books *(cont.)*

The people felt good after they ate their dinners. They started to fall asleep during the concert.

3

The people were surprised by the loud chord. Haydn was happy that he was able to keep them awake.

4

66

Sample Plans—*The Clock Symphony*

Day 1: Once again, show students the picture of the composer, Franz Joseph Haydn (page 62). Remind students that Haydn wrote the *Surprise Symphony*. Explain that he also wrote a piece of music called *The Clock Symphony.*

Show students a clock and a watch. Compare/contrast the clock and watch. Bring to class samples of different types of clocks. Discuss the different parts, such as the face, minute hand, and hour hand. Compare/contrast different types of clock faces. Tell students that long ago time was measured using a sundial. You may wish to have students create sundials to show them how shadows were used to tell the time of day. Explain to students that there are 24 hours in a day. Point out that the first twelve hours are A.M. and the later twelve hours are P.M. Play the recording of *The Clock Symphony.* Ask students to listen for the "tick-tock" sound of a clock.

Day 2: Ask students to name the composer of the *Surprise Symphony* and *The Clock Symphony.* If they cannot recall Haydn's name, provide it for them. Summarize the biographical information. Play the recording of *The Clock Symphony.* Have students raise their hands when they hear the "tick-tock" sound of the clock. Then, replay the recording, and ask them to clap to the "tick-tock" beat. Tell students that the clock sound is made by string instruments. Show them pictures of a violin, viola, cello, and double bass. Review the fact that each of these instruments has four strings.

Help students learn to tell time using the clock in your classroom. Play the recording of *The Clock Symphony* to introduce your lesson on telling time. Ask students to tell what time they do certain activities during the day, such as wake up, go to bed, and watch their favorite TV shows.

If possible take apart a clock. Allow students to see how the clock works. Explain that some clocks run on electricity while others use batteries. Show students the different sizes of batteries that are used to operate clocks.

Sample Plans—*The Clock Symphony* (cont.)

Day 3: Review the names of the instruments that make the "tick-tock" sound during the music. Once again, show pictures of the string instruments. Ask volunteers to count the strings and the black knobs. Have students pretend to be musicians and play one of the string instruments.

Introduce a metronome. Show students how it can be used to mark the timing of different beats. Play the recording of *The Clock Symphony* with the metronome. Call students' attention to the timing of the music.

Replay the recording and have students use the beat of the music to swing their arms back and forth like a pendulum on a clock. Then have them clap out the rhythm. You may wish to allow students to create dances to the beat of the music.

Provide white construction paper to students. Have students cut out pictures of clocks from magazines and newspapers and glue them onto their construction paper to create collages. Display the collages.

Day 4: Give each student a toy instrument. Play the recording of *The Clock Symphony*. Ask students to play the instruments only when they hear the "tick-tock" sound.

Review the job of a conductor (pages 37–39). Demonstrate how a conductor might move a baton. Remind students about safety rules so they will not touch each other during this activity. Then, replay the recording and have them pretend to be conductors, using unsharpened pencils or rulers as batons. Point out to students that they should move their batons to the beat of the music.

Provide paints and paintbrushes. Have students wear smocks or old shirts. Ask them to work in groups to create murals while listening to *The Clock Symphony*. Have the groups tell about their murals, and then display the art work.

Sample Plans—*The Clock Symphony* (cont.)

Day 5: Play the recording of *The Clock Symphony*. Ask students to tap their feet every time they hear the "tick-tock" sound.

Write the words *same* and *different* on the chalkboard. Explain the meanings of these words. Have students identify examples of things in the classroom that are the same and those that are different. Match the clocks (page 70). Invite volunteers to tell how the clocks are the same and how they are different.

Send a note home to parents, asking them to help their children count the number of clocks that they have at home. Make a chart that shows how many clocks each student has. Then use the information in the chart to create a graph.

Review the parts of a clock. Then have students make their own clocks (page 71). Have students hang their clocks on the classroom wall. Show them how to change the time on their clocks by moving the hour and minute hands. At times throughout the day (such as lunch time, rest time, and recess), help students change the time on their clocks to reflect the real time.

Replay the recording of *The Clock Symphony*. Then teach students the following poem.

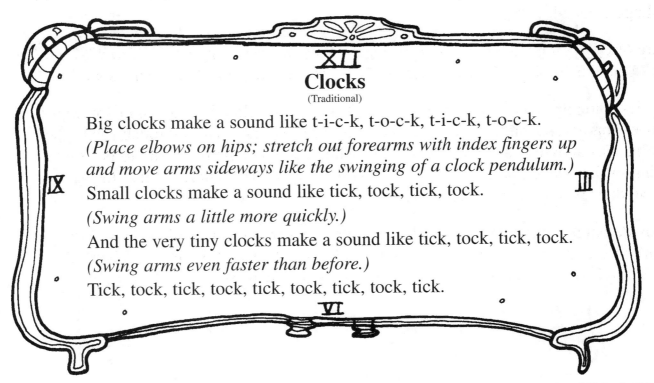

XII

Clocks
(Traditional)

Big clocks make a sound like t-i-c-k, t-o-c-k, t-i-c-k, t-o-c-k.
(Place elbows on hips; stretch out forearms with index fingers up and move arms sideways like the swinging of a clock pendulum.)
Small clocks make a sound like tick, tock, tick, tock.
(Swing arms a little more quickly.)
And the very tiny clocks make a sound like tick, tock, tick, tock.
(Swing arms even faster than before.)
Tick, tock, tick, tock, tick, tock, tick, tock, tick.

IX   III
VI

Match the Clocks

Look at the different types of clocks. Cut on the dotted lines. Glue each clock next to the one that it matches. Color the matching clocks.

Make a Clock

Look at a clock. Cut out and glue the numbers in the correct places on the circle to make it look like a clock. Cut out the clock and glue it on a piece of poster board. Allow the glue to dry. Draw a picture on your clock. Cut out the clock hands. Carefully punch a hole in the clock hands and the clock. Use a brad to connect the hands to the clock.

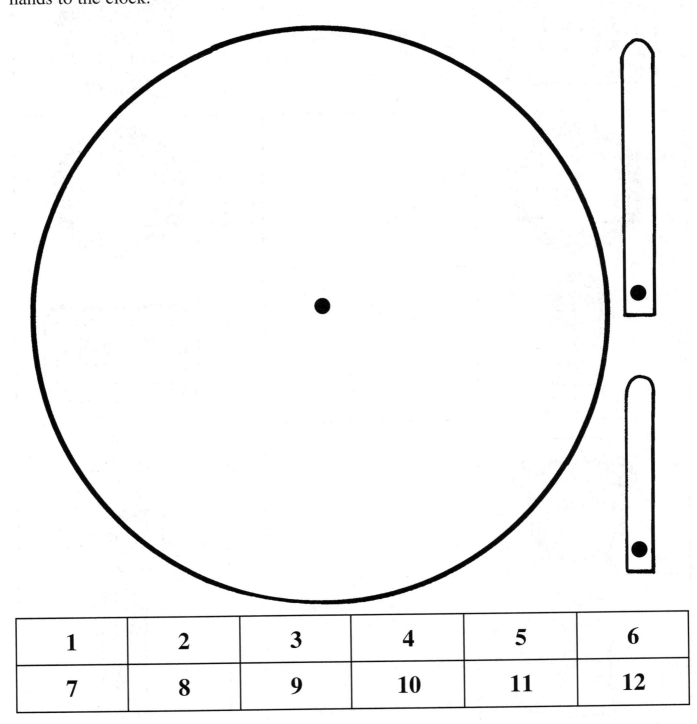

1	2	3	4	5	6
7	8	9	10	11	12

Sample Plans

Teacher Information: At one time there was some controversy over who wrote *The Toy Symphony*—Leopold Mozart or Franz Joseph Hadyn. However, a manuscript was discovered that confirmed that Mozart was the composer.

Day 1: Show students the picture of the composer Leopold Mozart (page 75) and read aloud the biographical sketch. Introduce and review the following instruments that are played in the *Toy Symphony:* drum, rattle, trumpet, horn, violin, bass violin. Some recordings include a triangle. If yours does, show students what the musical instrument called a triangle looks like. Explain that it gets its name from its shape. Show students that a triangle has three sides and three corners. Ask students to name other things that are shaped like a triangle.

Tell students that the *Toy Symphony* includes some toy instruments. Whistles are used to represent some birds. Take students on a walk outside the school and have them look for birds, nests, and eggs. Play the recording of *The Toy Symphony*. Ask students to raise the pictures of instruments that they hear. Then, replay the recording. Have students identify how many different types of whistles they hear. Lead students to conclude that there are three types of whistles.

Day 2: Play the recording of the *Toy Symphony*. Remind students that there are three types of bird whistles heard in the recording. Make an idea web with the word *birds* in the middle. Ask students to describe birds, and write their responses in surrounding circles.

Sample Idea Web

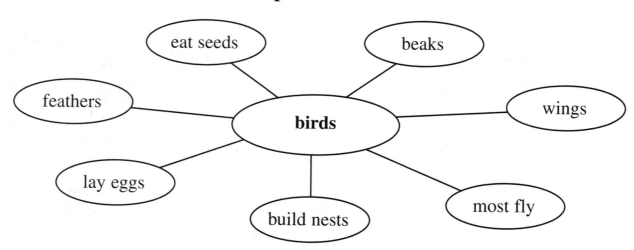

Show students pictures of cuckoos, quails, and nightingales. If possible, show students a cuckoo clock. Have them make the stick puppets (page 78). Play the recording. Model how to hold up each puppet when that bird is heard.

Sample Plans *(cont.)*

Day 3: Have students make bird pictures using dried lima beans. Split the lima beans in half. Have students glue down the bean halves. Tell them that the beans are the birds' bodies. Have them draw beaks and legs onto their beans. Encourage them to add backgrounds to their pictures.

Have students make birdseed rattles. Have them spoon some birdseed into paper cups. Cover the tops of the cups with butcher paper. Tape the butcher paper onto the cups. Play the recording of the *Toy Symphony* and have students shake their rattles to the beat of the music.

Have students make bird feeders (page 79). Hang them on some trees near the school. Allow students to sit and watch birds come to the feeders. Ask them to describe the types of birds that they see.

Day 4: Play the recording of the *Toy Symphony*. Remind students that one of the birds that can be heard whistling is called a cuckoo. Have them try to whistle like a cuckoo. Then teach students the following poem.

The Cuckoo

(Traditional)

In April

Come he will.

In flow'ry May

He sings all day.

In leafy June

He changes his tune.

In bright July

He's ready to fly.

In August

Go he must.

Sample Plans *(cont.)*

Day 5: If possible bring a real bird's nest to show students. Talk about how a nest is the bird's home. Have students compare/contrast the nest to their homes. Explain that the mother bird lays eggs in the nest and that baby birds hatch from the eggs. Then have students count the eggs in the nests (page 76) and make noodle nests (page 77). You can also have students do an eggshell art activity. Remove and clean the eggshells, dye them, and crush them into small pieces. After they are dry, allow students to use them to create pictures.

Divide the class into three groups—cuckoos, quails, and nightingales. Have students pretend to be that type of bird. Before playing the recording of the *Toy Symphony,* tell them to pretend to be sleeping when their type of bird is not heard and wake up when their type of bird is heard. Then play the recording.

Provide each student with a large blank index card. Ask students to cut out and glue down pictures of birds from magazines onto both sides of their index cards. Punch holes in the tops of the cards and use yarn to create some class mobiles.

Have students use paper plates to make birds. For each bird students will need the following: one paper plate for the body, the center of a paper plate for the head, a little less than half of a paper plate for the wing, and a small section of a plate for the tail. Have students use tempera paint and sponges to decorate their birds' feathers. Ask them to draw eyes and beaks. Then, display the birds.

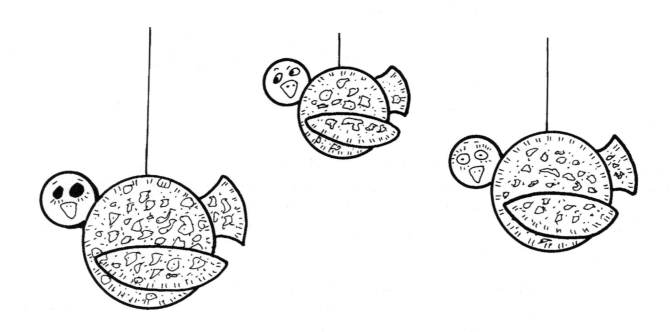

About the Composer

Leopold Mozart was born in 1719 in Germany. He played the violin and composed music. When he was 34 years old, he became a court composer. A few years later, he worked as an assistant conductor. By 1777, he was a teacher at a choir school. His compositions included oratorios; symphonies; operas; church music; piano, organ, and violin music; and trio sonatas.

Mozart had two children, Maria Anna and Wolfgang Amadeus. Both of his children were musically talented, but Wolfgang was especially gifted. Mozart took his young son on tour to play for many people, including royalty.

Count the Eggs

Count the eggs in each nest. Write the correct number in the box.

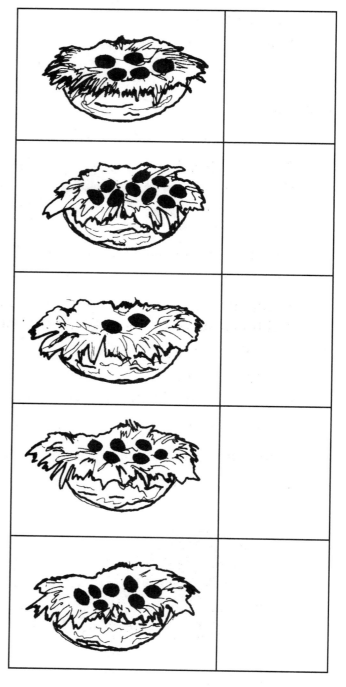

Noodle Nests

Have an adult help you follow the directions shown below to make a nest that you can eat!

Ingredients:

- 1 can frosting
- 4 cups (1 L) chow mein noodles
- jelly beans, small

Directions:

1. Place waxed paper on a cookie sheet.

2. Spoon the frosting into a saucepan. Place the saucepan on the stove over low heat. Frequently stir the frosting until it becomes liquid.

3. Turn off the stove.

4. Pour the noodles into the liquid frosting. Stir the noodles until they are covered with frosting.

5. Scoop up and place 1/4 cup (60 mL) of the noodles on the waxed paper. Place additional scoops of noodles on the waxed paper, making sure they are about 1 inch (2.54 cm) apart.

6. Use the back of a large spoon to make a hollow in each scoop of noodles. The hollows will be the middles of the nests.

7. Place 3–5 small jelly beans in each nest.

8. Allow the nests to cool until they are firm.

Stick Puppets

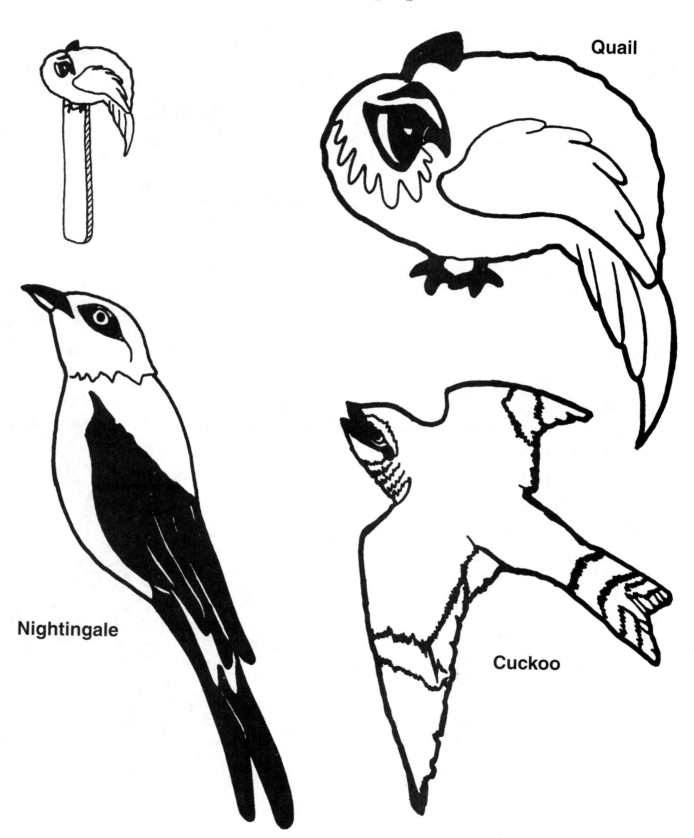

Quail

Nightingale

Cuckoo

78

Bird Feeder

Follow the directions shown below to make a bird feeder.

Materials:

- pine cone
- string or ribbon
- 1/4 cup (60 mL) peanut butter
- 1/4 cup (60 mL) bread crumbs
- 1 cup (250 mL) bird seed
- large bowl
- wooden spoon
- plastic knife

Directions:

1. Tie a long loop of string or ribbon onto the top of the pine cone.

2. Use the wooden spoon to mix the peanut butter and bread crumbs in the bowl. Continue stirring until the mixture is smooth.

3. Use the plastic knife and wooden spoon to spread the peanut butter mixture all over the pine cone.

4. Place the pine cone in some bird seed and roll it around. You may need to add more bird seed to the pine cone by pressing it on with your fingers.

5. Now use the loop at the top of the pine cone to hang the bird feeder on the branch of a tree.

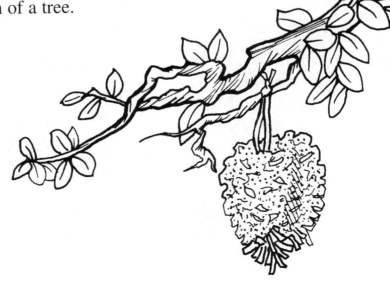

Sample Plans

Day 1: Show students the picture of the composer Wolfgang Amadeus Mozart (page 83) and read aloud the biographical sketch. Locate Austria on a map and show students where it is in relationship to your community. Play the recording and ask students if the song sounds familiar. Lead students to conclude that it is "Twinkle, Twinkle Little Star." Explain that Mozart wrote twelve variations on the theme of "Twinkle, Twinkle Little Star." Tell students that a variation means that the music will be a little different each time. If possible obtain two versions of the recording—one with Igor Kipnis playing the harpsichord and the other with Jorg Demus playing the piano. Point out that Mozart learned how to play the harpsichord at a very young age. Show students pictures of harpsichords and pianos. After students listen to the two recordings, ask them to compare/contrast the instruments.

Have students make little books (pages 84–88). Read the story to them. Explain that this story is a biography because it tells about Mozart's life. Discuss the sequence of events in the story. Then have students role-play the story.

Discuss the difference between an autobiography and a biography. Then take your class to the library and show students how to locate a biography about Mozart. Read the book to students.

Day 2: Show students a variety of star pictures. Tell students that many people like to wish on stars. Write the words to the traditional "Twinkle, Twinkle Little Star" on the chalkboard or a chart. Teach students the words and invite them to sing the song for other classes. Then, have students pretend that if they make a wish on a star, it will come true. Play the recording and ask students to draw pictures of the things they would wish for.

Trace the star pattern (page 89) onto poster board for students. Punch holes around the edges of the poster board stars. Provide yarn for students to lace the sides of their poster board stars. As an alternative to this activity, you can have students place toothpicks to cover the poster board star.

Sample Plans (cont.)

Day 3: Play the recording of the "Twinkle, Twinkle Little Star" variations. Help students recognize when different variations begin by asking them to raise their hands each time a new one is heard.

Cut sponges into different sized stars. Allow students to use tempera paint, construction paper, and the sponge stars to create pictures. Read aloud a story about stars as students are working on their pictures. Display the pictures in the classroom. You may wish to create a learning center with books about stars on a table and their stars hanging on the wall next to the table.

Introduce the following terms: solo, duet, trio, and quartet (page 90). Have students use the instruments that they have made in this unit or real instruments to role-play performing a solo, duet, trio, and quartet.

Day 4: Trace the star pattern (page 89) onto tagboard. Make two tagboard stars for each student. Help students cut slits in their stars so that they can be joined together to make three-dimensional stars. Punch a hole in one point of each star and tie a loop of yarn or ribbon through the hole. Hang up the stars.

Play a recording called *Rondo Alla Turca*. It is the Sonata in A Major. This is a lively piece of music. Play the music first and then have students march in rhythm to the beat. March around the room once more, this time clapping hands to the beat.

Sample Plans (cont.)

Day 5: Play Haydn's the *Surprise Symphony* for students. Remind students that the story behind this symphony is that Haydn wanted to awaken people who were asleep during his performance. Then play the third selection on a recording entitled the *Comic Mozart.* It is a takeoff on the *Surprise Symphony* composed by Joseph Haydn. Mozart has a chorus of people singing "Hush, hush, step quietly. Do not make any noise," while his music sounds like the main theme of the *Surprise Symphony.* Where the loud chord is usually played in Haydn's symphony, Mozart has a musician gently hit a timpani with a mallet.

Play the minuet entitled *Allegro Assai-Andante-Minuetto.* Explain to students that a minuet is a type of music that people used to dance to long ago. Show the picture of the people dancing in Mozart's time (page 88). Call students' attention to the mode of dress and how the people dancing are holding their arms as they move to the music. Remind students to watch where they are going so they do not run into other partners in the circle.

You may wish to extend this activity using the following activities:

- After the music has been heard a few times, teach students to sing "La, La, La" with the melody.

- Have students stand in a circle with partners. Have students face each other and stand as shown in the picture on page 88. Then have them walk around the circle in rhythm to the music.

- When the children feel comfortable moving to this music, they can use other dance steps. For instance, they can learn how to turn around in a circle and then rejoin hands. You may wish to have students sing the melody while dancing.

Mozart's birthday is on January 25. Write a note home asking parents to help their children find the number on a radio dial for a classical music station. (If school is in session on that day, bring a radio to class for students.) Tell students to listen to that station on January 25. Ask them to see if they can tell which famous composer's birthday it is. Then discuss with students that it is Mozart's birthday.

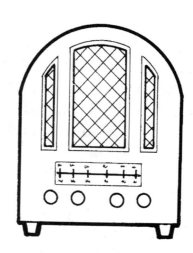

About the Composer

Wolfgang Amadeus Mozart was born in Salzburg, Austria, in 1756. Mozart seemed to be like any other baby until he was about three years old. At that age, he pretended to play the clavier like his sister, Maria Anna. When he was four years old, he learned to play the violin and started making up his own music. By the time he was six, he was giving concerts all over Europe.

Mozart wrote symphonies and an opera when he was only eight. He was a musical genius. He wrote music quickly and easily. Unfortunately, he was frequently sick. Mozart spent 14 years traveling and giving concerts. This made his health even worse. During his short lifetime, Mozart wrote many pieces of music, including 41 symphonies, 27 quartets, 30 string quartets, and more than 200 cantatas. Mozart died in 1791.

Making Little Books

Wolfgang Amadeus Mozart

Name _____

Wolfgang Amadeus Mozart is born in Salzburg, Austria, in 1756.

2

Making Little Books *(cont.)*

Papa Mozart looks at Wolfgang in his cradle.

3

Wolfgang kisses Papa on the tip of his nose every night before going to bed.

4

Making Little Books *(cont.)*

Wolfgang likes to hear the clock saying "Tick-tock, tick-tock."

5

Wolfgang does not like to hear the organ played so loudly.

6

Making Little Books *(cont.)*

Wolfgang listens to the harpsichord, thinking about all the music he wants to play.

7

Mama and Papa Mozart come running into the music room.

Wolfgang can reach the keys of the harpsichord!

8

Making Little Books *(cont.)*

Wolfgang plays quartets with Papa and his friends.

9

Wolfgang writes many wonderful pieces of music.

Many people like dancing to Wolfgang's music.

10

Star Pattern

Types of Musical Compositions

Solo—A piece of music for one person

Duet—A piece of music for two people

Trio—A piece of music for three people

Quartet—A piece of music for four people

Sample Plans

Day 1: Show students the picture of the composer Paul Dukas (page 94) and read aloud the biographical sketch. Locate France on a world map and show students where it is in relationship to your community.

Tell students that Dukas composed a piece of music entitled *The Sorcerer's Apprentice.* Explain that a sorcerer is a person who makes magic things happen and an apprentice is a person who helps do the work of the sorcerer. Tell students that this story is about a young boy who gets a job working for a man who does magic things. Therefore, the young boy is called "The Sorcerer's Apprentice."

If possible do some simple magic tricks for your class or hire a professional magician to perform for students. Ask students to tell about magic tricks that they have seen. Invite them to draw pictures of magicians performing tricks.

Read aloud "The Story of the Sorcerer's Apprentice" (pages 97–99). Then play the recording of *The Sorcerer's Apprentice.* You may wish to read aloud the story while playing the recording.

Day 2: Review "The Story of the Sorcerer's Apprentice" (pages 97–99). Ask volunteers to retell the events of the story. Help students make hats (page 105). Introduce the word *imagination.* Explain to students what *imagination* is. Ask half the class to imagine they are the sorcerer and wear their hats. Ask the other half of the class to imagine they are the apprentice. Have students role-play the events while listening to the recording. Allow the groups to switch roles. Replay the recording and have students role-play the different roles.

When the music begins, the tempo is slow and the volume low. Play the recording of *The Sorcerer's Apprentice.* Call students' attention to the tempo and volume of the music. Ask them what events might be happening at different points in the music. For example, lead students to conclude that the music sounds as though the sorcerer is doing his magic or the apprentice is commanding the broom to bring in the buckets of water.

Sample Plans (cont.)

Day 3: Make little books (pages 100–104) with students. Read the story to students. Ask volunteers to retell the story. Stress the importance of telling the events in the order they occurred. Encourage students to share their little books with family members.

Divide the class into groups of three. In each group, have one student be the sorcerer, one be the apprentice, and one be the broom. Play the recording of *The Sorcerer's Apprentice* and have students dramatize the story. Allow students to use simple props and costumes. You may wish to narrate the story as students dramatize it. Invite other classes to watch the dramatizations.

Point out that at the very end of the music, there is a chord played that is loud and definite in its meaning. This chord consists of three notes that make you feel as though the sorcerer is saying, "And that is the end of that." Call students' attention to these three notes and suggest that they brush their hands together signifying the end of a chapter in the life of the apprentice.

Introduce the word *pantomime* and explain its meaning. Play *The Sorcerer's Apprentice* and have students pantomime the magic that the sorcerer is doing. After the music is over, ask them to tell you what kind of magic they were doing.

Day 4: Play the recording of *The Sorcerer's Apprentice*. Ask volunteers to tell what is happening at different points in the music. Divide the class into small groups. Provide a piece of butcher paper for each group. Then replay the recording. As students listen to the music, ask them to paint a mural that shows something from the story. Discuss the order of events depicted by the murals. Then display the murals along the classroom walls in the order that the events of the story occurred.

Review the job that a conductor does. Allow students to pretend to be conductors while the recording is playing. Remind students to carefully move their batons (unsharpened pencils or rulers).

Sample Plans *(cont.)*

Day 5: Play the recording of *The Sorcerer's Apprentice*. Obtain a copy of the Walt Disney video *Fantasia*. See the Technology Bibliography (page 143) for information. Fast forward to *The Sorcerer's Apprentice*. Play that segment of the video for students. Ask students to tell about the events shown in the video. Reread the story (pages 97–99). Have students compare/contrast the events in the story with those in the video.

Write the word *feelings* inside of a circle on the chalkboard. Ask students what kinds of feelings (emotions) they have. Create a word web with students' responses.

Sample Word Web

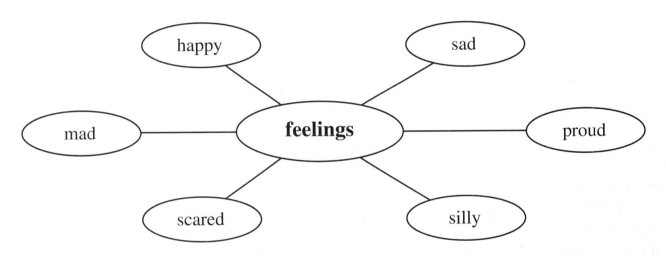

Have them tell how the characters felt during the following events:
- How the apprentice felt when he got the job
- How the apprentice felt when the sorcerer would not let him do any magic
- How the sorcerer felt about doing magic
- How the sorcerer felt about the apprentice before the flood
- How the apprentice felt when he did the magic
- How the apprentice felt when the broom started bringing too much water
- How the apprentice felt when he could not stop the flood
- How the sorcerer felt when he returned home to find the flood
- How the apprentice felt when the sorcerer discovered that he had been doing magic
- How they both felt at the end of the story

Ask students what they would have done if they had been the sorcerer or his apprentice.

About the Composer

Paul Dukas was born in Paris, France, in 1865. He went to school at the Paris Conservatory. While there, he won many prizes including the second Prix de Rome for his cantata called *Velleda*. He became a successful composer in 1892 by writing a concert overture. In 1897, Dukas introduced *The Sorcerer's Apprentice*. Audiences all over the world loved this piece of music.

In 1910, Dukas became a teacher at the Paris Conservatory. He continued to write music until 1912. However, he worked slowly and found that composing was very hard for him. Just weeks before his death in 1935, Dukas destroyed some of his later works. Today only a handful of his compositions still exist.

Paul Dukas

Flannel Board Patterns

Sorcerer

Bucket

Broom

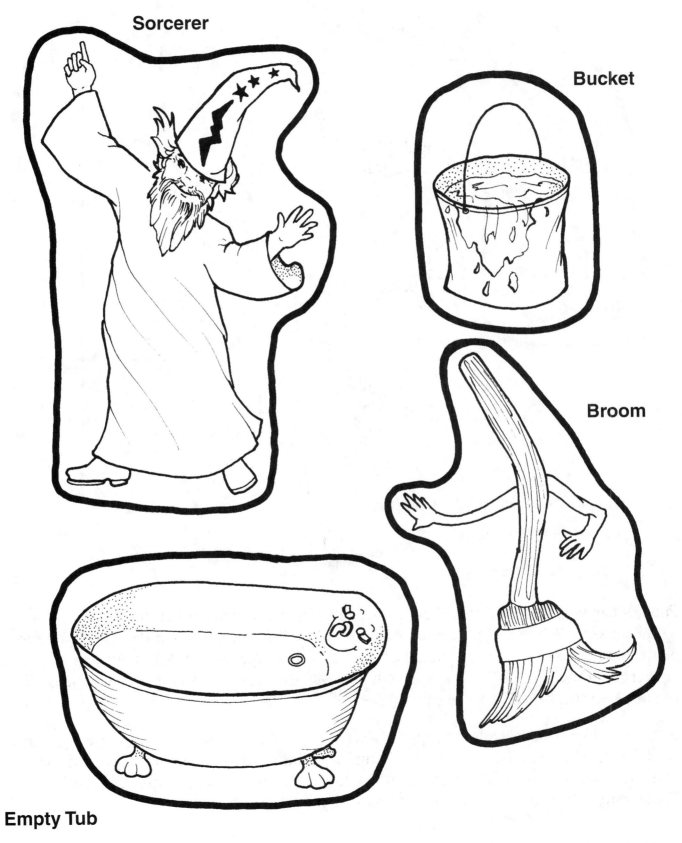

Empty Tub

Flannel Board Patterns *(cont.)*

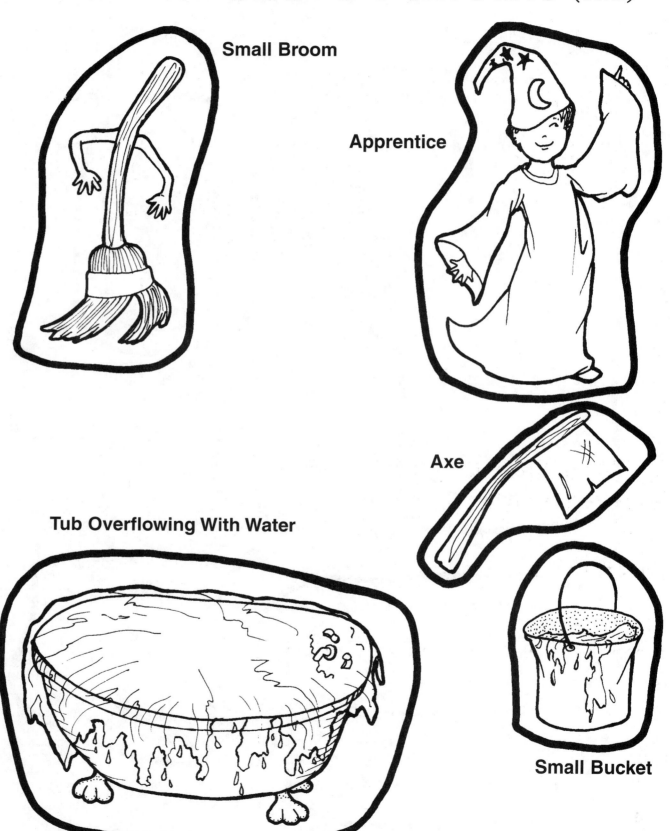

Small Broom

Apprentice

Axe

Tub Overflowing With Water

Small Bucket

96

The Story of the Sorcerer's Apprentice

A young boy was walking along the road when he spotted a sign near the door of a very big house. He looked closely at the sign and saw that it read "Apprentice needed to work with Sorcerer."

The boy immediately decided to find out what that job was so he rang the doorbell. A tall man with a long white beard opened the door. When the boy saw this odd-looking man, he jumped back.

The man asked, "What can I do for you, young man?"

The boy replied, "I was walking by and saw your sign by the door. I need a job, and I thought I would find out what being an apprentice is all about."

The sorcerer looked the boy over and said, "I need someone who will help me in my work. I do all kinds of magic. I can turn a bird into a cat and a small fish into a huge whale. Those are only a couple of examples of the magic things that I do. If you want the job, you must follow my directions, and you must never, ever try to do the magic tricks that I do. Some time in the future, I will teach you all the magic I know. I am an old man, and some day I will not be able to do my magic. When that day comes, you will become the next great sorcerer, and everyone will look to you for magical events."

The Story of the Sorcerer's Apprentice *(cont.)*

The boy was so happy that he jumped for joy and said, "Yes, yes, Master, I certainly do want to become your apprentice. I promise to obey all of your rules."

"Good," said the sorcerer. "Come in and we will start our work right away."

The boy walked into the big house and saw many strange and different things that he had never seen before. He did not know where to look first because there were so many things to see. The sorcerer walked beside the boy and asked, "Do you have a name?"

The boy said, "Yes, I do have a name. I am called Henry."

The sorcerer showed Henry where the work room was and what they would be doing for the rest of the day. Henry felt very happy.

Henry worked with the sorcerer for many days. He closely watched everything the sorcerer did. Soon Henry forgot that he had promised that he would not do any magic tricks that he saw the sorcerer do. Each day Henry would hide behind the door and listen to all the words the sorcerer said to make magical things happen. One day the sorcerer told Henry that he must go away for the day. He wanted Henry to have hot water in the tub so that he could bathe when he returned home. When the sorcerer left, Henry knew he had to go down to the river and carry many buckets of water up the long winding stairs before he could fill the tub up to the top. Suddenly Henry got an idea.

The Story of the Sorcerer's Apprentice *(cont.)*

Henry decided he would say some magic words so that a broom would take the bucket down to the river and come back with water for the tub. He then commanded the broom to get the buckets of water.

The broom made many trips to the river. Each time the broom returned, the bucket was filled with water. Within a short time, the tub was completely filled with water. Henry knew he had to do something quickly to stop the broom from bringing any more buckets of water. However, he could not think of the words that would put a stop to the magic. Now the water was spilling over the edge of the tub. Soon there was so much water that it covered Henry's shoes. Still the broom kept bringing more water. Henry grabbed an axe and tried to chop up the broom. But that just made little brooms. The little brooms brought more and more water. Soon the water rose up to Henry's arms. Poor Henry did not know what to do. Suddenly, Henry heard a sound. He was both frightened and thankful when he realized that it was the sorcerer, returning from his trip.

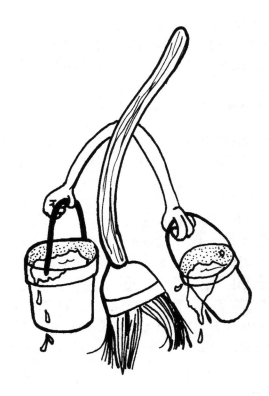

The sorcerer immediately realized what had happened. As a result, he quickly said the magic words needed to stop the brooms from bringing more water in the buckets. Now that things had calmed down, the sorcerer turned to Henry and said, "You did not remember a promise that you made to me when you first came here. You weren't supposed to try any magic until I told you you could."

Henry was ashamed that he had not kept his promise. He asked the sorcerer to forgive him. Once again Henry promised to do the right thing. He told the sorcerer that never again would he try to do magic when left alone to do his chores.

Making Little Books

The Sorcerer's Apprentice

Name _____

A young boy named Henry sees a sign on the door of a big house.

It says that the sorcerer needs an apprentice.

2

Making Little Books *(cont.)*

The sorcerer opens the door.

3

Henry promises not to do any of the sorcerer's magic tricks.

4

Making Little Books (cont.)

Henry hides and watches the sorcerer do his magic tricks.

5

Henry tells the broom to bring buckets of water for the tub.

6

Making Little Books (cont.)

The broom has brought so much water that the tub is overflowing.

7

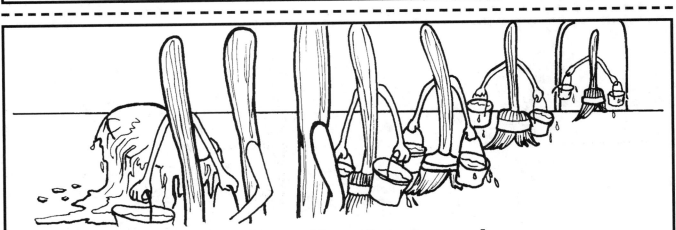

Henry tries to stop the broom by chopping it into little pieces. Now there are lots of little brooms. They keep bringing more water even though the entire house is flooded.

8

Making Little Books *(cont.)*

The sorcerer comes home and finds water everywhere.

9

The sorcerer puts everything back the way it was.

10

104

Make a Sorcerer's Hat

Make sorcerer's hats for students. Allow them to wear the hats as they role-play the story of *The Sorcerer's Apprentice*.

Use the following materials and directions for each hat.

Materials:

- 12 inches x 24 inches (30 cm x 61 cm) tagboard
- pencil
- scissors
- masking tape
- art supplies, such as crayons, markers, glitter, stickers, etc.

Directions:

1. Fold the piece of tagboard in half.
2. Use the pencil to draw a quarter circle on the folded piece of tagboard.
3. Cut along the line that you drew in Step 2.
4. Unfold the tagboard. You should have a half circle.
5. Use the tagboard half circle to make a cone that is large enough to fit a student's head.
6. Use masking tape to keep the cone together.
7. Allow the student to decorate his or her sorcerer's hat.

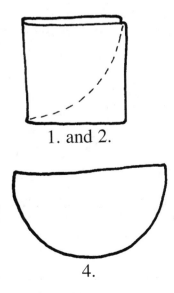

1. and 2.

4.

5. and 6.

7.

Sample Plans

Day 1: Show students the picture of the composer Camille Saint-Saëns (page 109) and read aloud the biographical sketch. Locate France on a world map and show students where it is in relationship to your community.

Tell students that Saint-Saëns composed *The Carnival of the Animals*. Explain to students what a carnival is. Then write the word *animals* in a circle on the chalkboard. Ask students to name animals. Create a word web by writing their responses in surrounding circles.

Sample Word Web

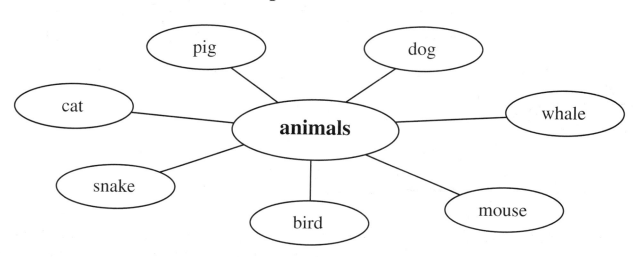

Preview the recording of *The Carnival of the Animals* to choose some selections that you think your students will enjoy and benefit from the most. For example, the selection entitled "The Swan" is very appropriate for young students. Ask students if they know what a swan is and what it looks like. Show them a picture. Point out the swan's long neck and how graceful the swan looks as it swims.

Play the recording of "The Swan" for students. Tell them that the solo instrument played is the cello. Show students a real cello or pictures of cellos. Explain that the cello represents the swan. Review with students that the cello is a string instrument. Ask them to count the number of strings and tuning pegs. Have students name the other instruments in the string family. *(violin, viola, double bass)* Remind students that the cello is used to play low notes.

Sample Plans *(cont.)*

Day 2: If possible, take a field trip to a local pond that has swans, geese, and/or ducks. Take loaves of bread, and allow students to feed the birds. Upon returning to the classroom, have students draw pictures of themselves feeding the swans, geese, and/or ducks. As an alternative field trip, take students to a zoo, nature center, wildlife park, etc. After returning to the classroom, have students draw pictures of their favorite animals.

Day 3: Read aloud some basic information about swans. Have students make swan models (page 113). Ask them to name the parts of a swan, such as the head, eyes, bill, neck, body, wings, feathers, legs, and feet. Display the swan models on a table.

Play the recording of "The Swan" from *The Carnival of the Animals*. Ask students to pretend they are graceful swans. Take photographs of students during this creative movement activity. Display the pictures on a bulletin board.

Day 4: Tell students that many different kinds of animals are portrayed in *The Carnival of the Animals*. Display the flannel board pieces (page 110) and ask students to name the animals. Have students match the fronts and backs of different animals (page 112).

Display books about a variety of animals. You may wish to present videos, songs, and poems that are about animals. Then, have students work together as a class to create some animal poetry. Allow them to illustrate the poems.

Discuss with students the needs that all animals share: food, water, shelter. Call the local humane society to see what kinds of things they need. Have your class sponsor a school drive to solicit donations for the animals at the shelter.

Sample Plans *(cont.)*

Day 5: Play the recording of "The Swan" from *The Carnival of the Animals.* Provide each student with a scarf or a long narrow strip of newspaper. Ask students to wave that paper or scarf as they dance around the room to the music. Remind them to follow safety rules when dancing. After playing the recording, ask students how many instruments were played. Lead students to conclude that only one instrument was heard. Remind students that music is called a solo when only one instrument is played. Review how many instruments play in a solo, duet, trio, and quartet.

Tell students about some of the other animals from *The Carnival of the Animals.* Make elephant hats (page 111) with students. Discuss how elephants move. Invite volunteers to show the class. Have students wear the elephant hats and move around, pretending to be elephants. Then tell students about kangaroos. Use a map to show students where Australia is in relationship to your community. Tell students that mother kangaroos carry their babies in a pouch. Have students make the kangaroo and joey (page 114). Tell students to pretend to be kangaroos as they move around the room.

Have a class carnival of the animals. Before doing this activity, check your school's policies about having live animals in the building. If animals are permitted, send a note home to parents inviting them to bring family pets to class. Stress that all pets must be on leashes, in carriers, or in cages. Allow students to tell the class about their pets. You may wish to schedule the date and time for parents to bring the pets so that only a few animals are brought each day.

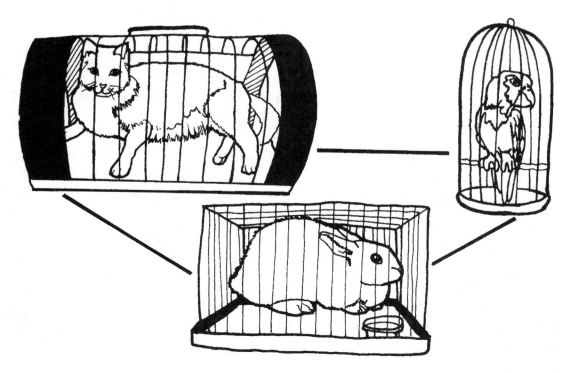

About the Composer

Camille Saint-Saëns was born in Paris, France, in 1835. He gave his first piano concert when he was ten years old. He went to school at the Paris Conservatory from the time he was thirteen until he graduated. He was given prizes for playing the organ as well as composing pieces of music.

People liked Saint-Saëns and they enjoyed his music. He was a very talented composer. He wrote many pieces of music, including five symphonies, 12 operas, several concertos, and over 100 songs. The *Danse Macabre, Samson and Delilah,* and *The Carnival of the Animals* are among his most popular compositions. In 1921, Saint-Saëns died while traveling in Algiers, Algeria.

Flannel Board Patterns

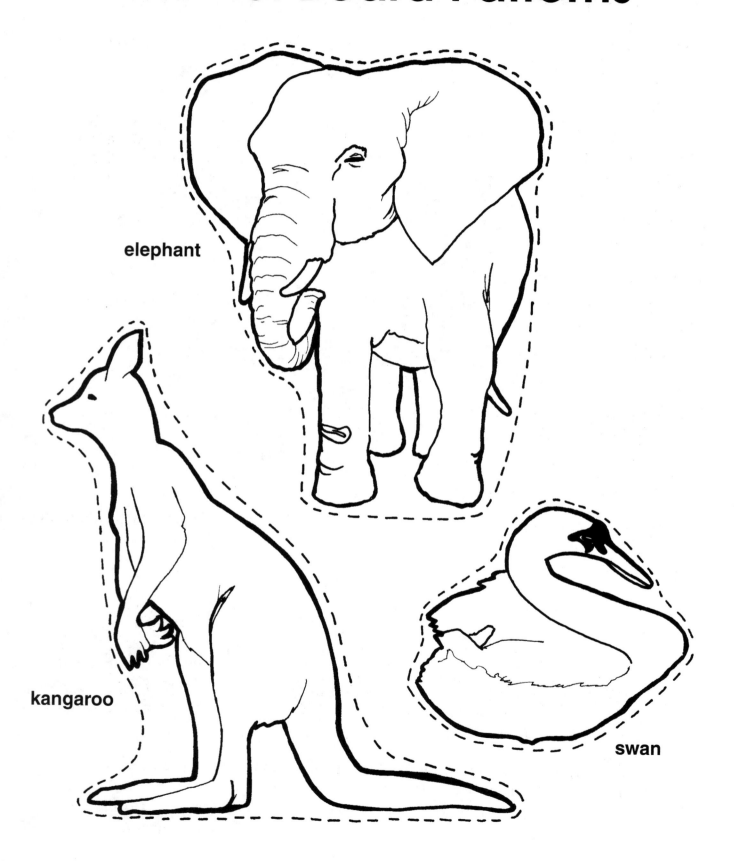

elephant

kangaroo

swan

Make an Elephant Hat

You can look like an elephant by making the hat described below. Have an adult or older student help you.

Materials:

- gray tagboard or tagboard that is painted gray
- gray construction paper
- scissors
- glue
- black crayon

Directions:

1. Use tagboard to make the tube that will fit around your head. Trim the tagboard so the ends overlap about one inch (2.54 cm). Use tape to keep the tube together.

2. Draw two large ears on gray construction paper. Cut them out.

3. Glue one ear to each side of the tube.

4. To make the trunk, cut a long strip of gray construction paper. Be sure one end is a little wider than the other end.

5. Fold the strip back and forth accordion style.

6. Glue the trunk in the middle of the tube's front.

7. Draw two eyes on the front of the tube. Be sure there is one eye on each side of the trunk.

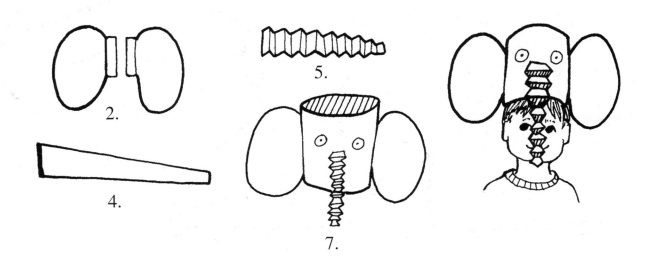

Camille Saint-Saëns

Match the Carnival Animals

Cut and paste. Then color the animals.

Make a Swan

Use the directions shown below to make a swan.

Materials:

- white poster board
- white feathers
- glue
- white pipe cleaners
- scissors

Directions:

1. Trace the shown circle below on a piece of poster board. Cut out the circle from the poster board. This circle will be the swan's body.

2. Carefully glue several feathers onto the poster board circle. These feathers will be the swan's wings, back, and tail.

3. Have an adult help you use scissors to scrape off 1/2 inch (1.25 cm) from one end of the pipe cleaner. This will be the swan's bill.

4. Bend the pipe cleaner to make the swan's head and neck. Glue the pipe cleaner onto the poster board circle.

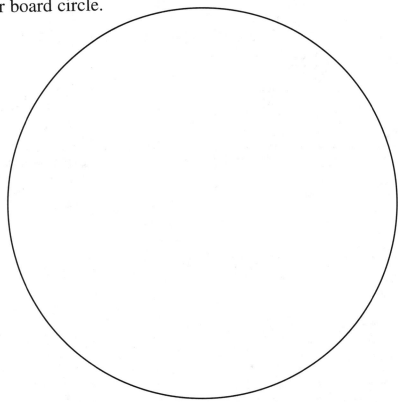

Kangaroos

Glue this page onto a piece of tagboard. Allow the glue to dry. Cut out the mother kangaroo, the pouch, and the joey (baby kangaroo). Staple the sides and bottom of the pouch onto the mother kangaroo. Leave the top of the pouch open. Place the joey inside the pouch.

joey

pouch

114

Sample Plans

Day 1: Show students the picture of the composer Nikolai Rimsky-Korsakov (page 118) and read aloud the biographical sketch. Locate Russia on a world map and show students where it is in relationship to your community. Tell students that Rimsky-Korsakov composed a piece of music entitled *The Flight of the Bumblebee.* Play the recording of this music. Point out to students that flutes are used to represent the bees. Review with students what a flute looks like and that it is a wind instrument. Ask them to name other wind instruments.

Read aloud information about bees. Explain how they gather nectar to make honey. Stress to students that bees can be dangerous because of their stingers. Ask them if they have ever been stung by bees.

Have students make bee costumes (page 119). Then play the recording. Have students pretend to be bumblebees, flying and buzzing around the classroom. Remind them to follow safety rules as they move. Encourage students to fly in circles, swoop up and down, stop to gather nectar from flowers, etc.

Day 2: Have students make little books that tell about bees (pages 122–125). Read aloud the book. Have students retell you the information given in the book. Play the recording of *The Flight of the Bumblebee* as students color the pages of their books.

Invite a beekeeper to speak to your students. Ask the guest to show some of the equipment and special clothing that beekeepers use. Take a poll to see if students would like to be beekeepers. Ask students what they would like and dislike about this type of job.

Sample Plans *(cont.)*

Day 3: Have students complete the flower art activity (page 120). Display a diagram of the parts of a flower. Remind students that bees fly from flower to flower in order to gather nectar. Explain how bees move pollen as they collect the nectar of different flowers. Show students some flowers on which the pollen is visible. Allow students to touch the pollen. Remind them not to eat it.

Tell students that bees use nectar to make honey. Show a picture of a beehive. Explain that the honey bees make is inside the hive. Bring some honey to class. Invite students to taste it. Make honey granola (page 121) for students to enjoy as a snack. Be sure to ask parents if their children have any food allergies or dietary restrictions.

Day 4: Play the recording of *The Flight of the Bumblebee* as students work on the following art activity. Provide white construction paper to students. Have students glue down poppy seeds, kernels of corn, and twigs to create flowers. The poppy seeds are for the inside of the flower, the corn kernels are for the petals, and the twig is for the stem.

Poppy Seed

Corn

Twig

Teach students the following poem and finger play.

Bumblebee

(Unknown)

Bee, bee, bumblebee
(Pretend there is a bee on the thumb by placing the index finger there.)

Sting a boy/girl upon his/her knee.
(Show the index finger "stinging" the knee.)

Sting the pig upon his snout,
(Show the index finger "stinging" the nose.)

One, two, three, four, five—you're out!
(Point at students as the numbers are said.)

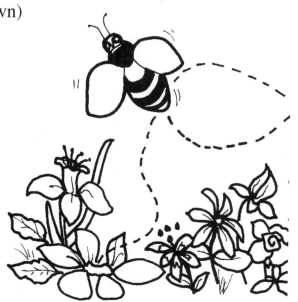

Sample Plans *(cont.)*

Day 5: Have students make bumblebees. For each student, trace the patterns shown below on construction paper as follows: one set of purple wings, two yellow circles, one red stinger. Paint a toilet paper roll with yellow tempera paint. Then use black tempera paint to add stripes. Draw a face on one yellow circle. Glue a yellow circle on each end of the tube. On the end of the tube that does not have the face, glue the stinger. Glue the wings onto the top of the tube. Cut thin strips of black construction paper to make three sets of legs. Glue the legs onto the bottom of the tube. After all students have completed their bumblebees, hang them from the ceiling.

About the Composer

Nikolai Rimsky-Korsakov was born in Russia in 1844. When he was three years old, he played the drum while his father played the piano. At the age of eight, he learned how to play the piano. One year later, he began writing his own music.

Rimsky-Korsakov studied at the Naval College located in St. Petersburg. During this time, he wrote symphonies, orchestral works, and his first opera. In 1869, he became a popular composer when his tone poem, "Sadko," was performed. He began working as a teacher at the St. Petersburg Conservatory. He continued his own studies of composition and instruments so that he could better understand all aspects of music.

Like other gifted composers, Rimsky-Korsakov wrote many pieces of music. His works included symphonies, operas, concertos, and chamber music. He continued to write compositions until he died in St. Petersburg in 1908.

Make a Bee Costume

Have parent volunteers help you make bee costumes for your students. You will need to gather enough materials and repeat the directions for the number of costumes you wish to make.

Materials:

- yellow poster board (2)
- yellow tagboard
- black tempera paint
- paintbrushes
- stapler
- black pipe cleaners (2)

Directions:

1. Draw two large circles on pieces of yellow poster board. Cut them out.

2. Paint black horizontal stripes across the circles. Allow the paint to dry.

3. Cut two strips of yellow tagboard that are about one inch (2.54 cm) wide and at least ten inches (25 cm) long.

4. Staple the two strips of tagboard to make a sandwich board from the poster board circles.

5. Make a headband by cutting a strip of yellow tagboard that is two inches (5 cm) wide and long enough to go around a student's head. Be sure the ends overlap about one inch (2.54 cm).

6. Staple the headband together where the ends overlap. Cut off any excess tagboard.

7. Make antennae by slightly bending one end of each pipe cleaner.

8. Staple the straight ends of the pipe cleaners to the front of the headband.

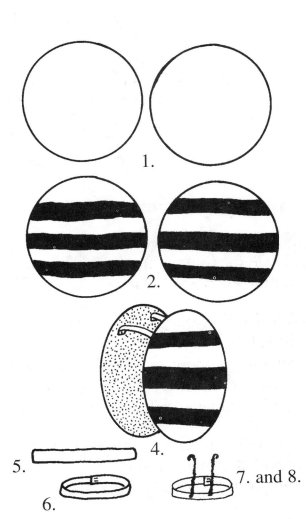

Flower Art

Use the following directions to make an art project with flowers.

Materials: plate, 6 inches (15 cm) in diameter; clear contact paper; pencil; scissors; pressed flowers; plastic tape, any color; hole puncher; ribbon or yarn

Directions:

1. With the backing still on the contact paper, use the plate to trace two circles.
2. Cut out the circles.
3. Take off the backing from one circle. Lay it on the table with the sticky side up.
4. Place some pressed flowers on the sticky side of the circle. Be sure some flowers face toward you while others face away.
5. Take off the backing from the other circle.
6. Place the two sticky sides of the circles together.
7. Squeeze the circles together. Place a heavy book on top of them for several minutes.
8. Use plastic tape to seal the edges of the circles.
9. Use the hole puncher to make a hole in the top of the circles.
10. Use ribbon or yarn to make a loop through the hole.

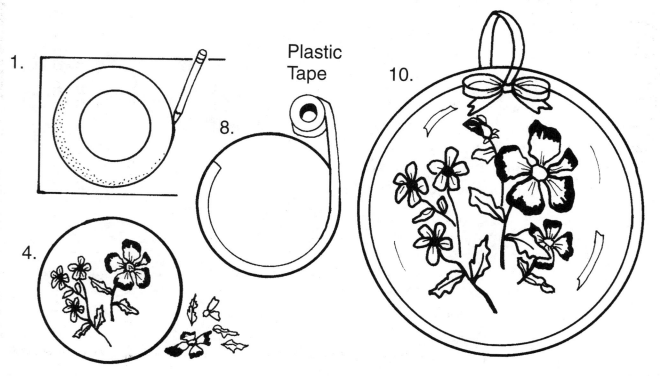

Honey Granola Recipe

Make some honey granola for your students to enjoy. Be sure to ask parents if their children have any food allergies or dietary restrictions.

Ingredients:

3 cups (750 mL) rolled oats

1 cup (250 mL) coconut, shredded

3/4 cup (175 mL) wheat germ

3/4 cup (175 mL) nuts, chopped

3/4 cup (175 mL) soy beans

1/2 cup (125 mL) sunflower seeds

1/3 cup (83 mL) cooking oil

1/3 cup (83 mL) honey

1/2 teaspoon (2.5 mL) vanilla

1/2 teaspoon (2.5 mL) salt

Directions:

Preheat the oven to 300° F (150° C). In a large bowl, mix the rolled oats, shredded coconut, wheat germ, chopped nuts, soy beans, and sunflower seeds. Then stir in the cooking oil, honey, vanilla, and salt. Mix thoroughly. Spread the granola on a cooking tray. Place the tray in the oven. Stir frequently. Bake until crispy. Remove from the oven and allow the granola to cool before serving.

Making Little Books

A BOOK ABOUT BEES

Name _____

Bees live in a nest called a hive.

1

122

Making Little Books (cont.)

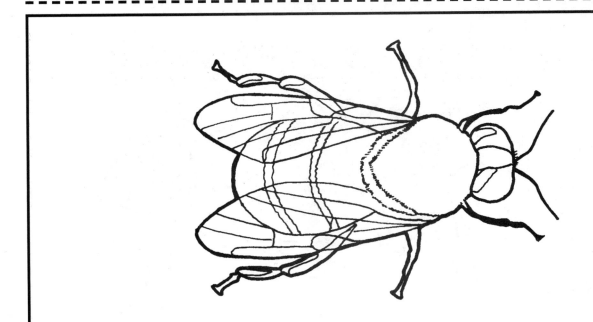

The drones are the male bees.

2

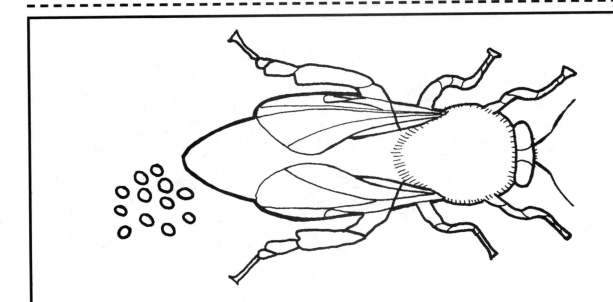

The queen bee is a female. She lays the eggs.

3

123

Making Little Books *(cont.)*

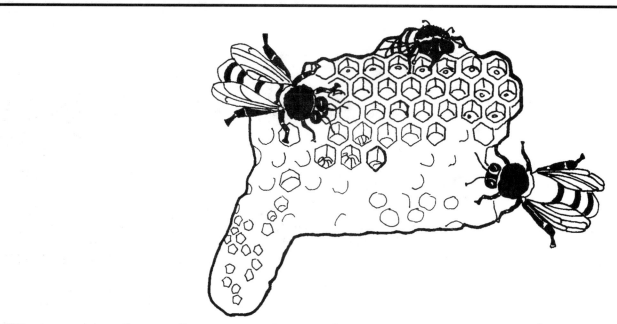

The worker bees are females. They take care of the hive.

4

Worker bees look for flowers that are full of nectar.

5

Making Little Books *(cont.)*

When a worker bee finds some flowers that are full of nectar, it returns to the hive and does a dance. The dance tells the other worker bees where the good flowers are.

6

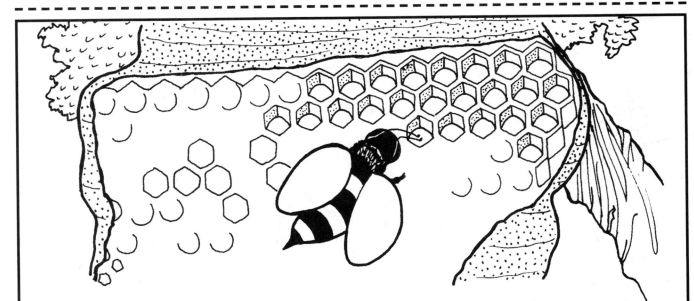

The worker bees use the nectar to make honey. They store the honey in the wax cells of the combs, or nest.

7

Sample Plans

Day 1: Show students the picture of the composer Ludwig van Beethoven (page 129) and read aloud the biographical sketch. Locate Germany on a world map and show students where it is in relationship to your community. Tell students that Beethoven composed a piece of music called *Symphony No. 6*, or the *Pastoral Symphony*. Explain that this symphony has five parts.

Write the word *sounds* in a circle on the chalkboard. Ask students to name everyday sounds that they hear. Create a word web by writing their responses in surrounding circles.

Sample Word Web

music   talking   car horn

telephone ringing   **sounds**   doorbell

dog barking   laughing   birds singing

Tell students that Beethoven began to lose his hearing as a young man. Discuss the problems a person who cannot hear might have. Make a two-column chart on the chalkboard with the headings *Inside Sounds* and *Outside Sounds*. Have students listen for sounds inside the classroom. Write a list of these sounds on the chart. Then take students outside and ask them to listen for sounds. Write a list of these sounds on the chart. Ask students which sounds they would miss the most.

Introduce the term *hearing impaired*. If possible arrange a field trip to a school for the hearing impaired. Explain that some hearing impaired people know how to spell words with their fingers. Teach students the manual alphabet (page 131). You may wish to help them learn how to spell their names using the manual alphabet.

Sample Plans (cont.)

Day 2: Tell students that Beethoven loved spending time in the country, walking through fields and seeing all the different birds. Even though he could not hear the sounds that were going on around him, he was able to imagine them in his mind. One day as Beethoven walked along a country road, he got an idea for a symphony. This was to be his sixth symphony which was named the *Pastoral Symphony*. Play the beginning of the recording. Ask students to imagine walking down a country road and seeing fields of flowers, trees, birds, etc. Have students move creatively to the music. Remind them to follow safety rules as they move.

Provide white construction paper, scissors, glue, muffin cups (paper liners), tissue paper, and markers or crayons for students to make flowers using the following directions. Cut slits in some of the muffin cups so the cups can be spread out. Smear glue on the bottom outside surface of the slit muffin cups. Glue the cups onto the construction paper. Then smear glue on the bottom outside surface of the other muffin cups. Glue these whole cups inside the ones with the slits. Cut small pieces of tissue paper and crush them. Glue the crushed tissue paper into the centers of the muffin cups. Draw a stem and leaves for each flower.

Day 3: Discuss the four seasons with students. Play the beginning of the recording of the *Pastoral Symphony*. Point out that this symphony represents events that take place in the spring. Then have students create a class collage by cutting out spring pictures from magazines and gluing them onto a large piece of butcher paper.

Sample Plans *(cont.)*

Day 4: Play the middle of the second half of the recording of the *Pastoral Symphony*. At first the music sounds like the beginning of the symphony. Then the tempo and mood change. Point out that the louder chords indicate that a storm is brewing. Ask students to imagine a darkening sky, trees bending in the wind, leaves falling to the ground, thunder, and lightning. When the music changes back to being softer, the storm is over.

Discuss the dangers of lightning with students. Then use the following demonstration to create a small amount of harmless lightning. Fold a large piece of thick plastic in half and securely tape it to the top of a table. Make a handle by attaching some modeling clay to the inside of a metal bowl. Darken the room as much as possible. Hold onto the clay, press hard, and slide the metal bowl across the piece of plastic several times. Slightly lift one end of the bowl. Then hold the metal object very close to the metal bowl. As static electricity is discharged, a small spark of lightning will appear.

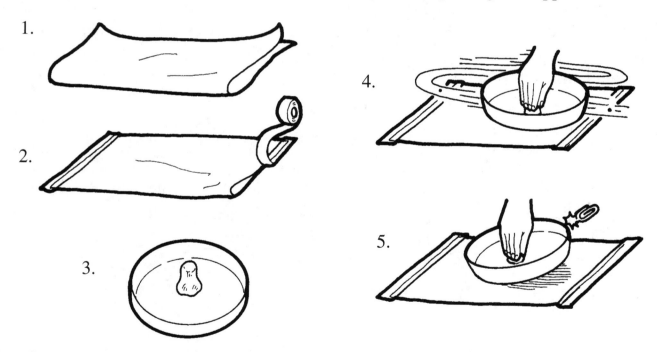

Day 5: Provide white construction paper and crayons for students. Show students how to fold their papers in half and draw lines down the middle. Tell students that they are going to draw two pictures: one that shows the countryside during a storm and the other that shows it after the storm. Play the storm part of the *Pastoral Symphony*. Have students draw their pictures while the music is playing.

Review with the class that Beethoven was an excellent pianist. Have students put together the piano puzzle (page 130).

About the Composer

Ludwig van Beethoven was born in Bonn, Germany, in 1770. By the time he was four, his father was teaching him how to play the piano and violin. His father wanted him to be a musical genius like Wolfgang Amadeus Mozart. As a result, his father would hit Beethoven on the knuckles with a cane whenever he made a mistake while practicing.

By the age of 12, Beethoven was working as an organist, pianist, and violinist. When he was 22, he moved to Vienna. While there, he became one of Franz Joseph Haydn's students. He spent his time teaching music lessons and writing compositions. When Beethoven was in his early thirties, his work became very popular. Unfortunately, it was during this time that he realized he was losing his hearing. By the time he was 50, he could hear only a buzzing sound. He refused to let this stop him. He continued to compose and conduct, hearing the music inside his head rather than with his ears. In 1827, just two years after Beethoven's last appearance in public, he died. He is best known for the nine symphonies he composed.

Piano Puzzle

For each student, glue a copy of the puzzle onto a piece of poster board. Allow students to color their copies of the puzzle. Laminate the puzzles or cover them with clear contact paper. Cut apart the pieces. Place each set in a reclosable plastic bag or an envelope for students to take home. Have students work with family members to put their puzzles together. Encourage students to tell their families what they have learned about music.

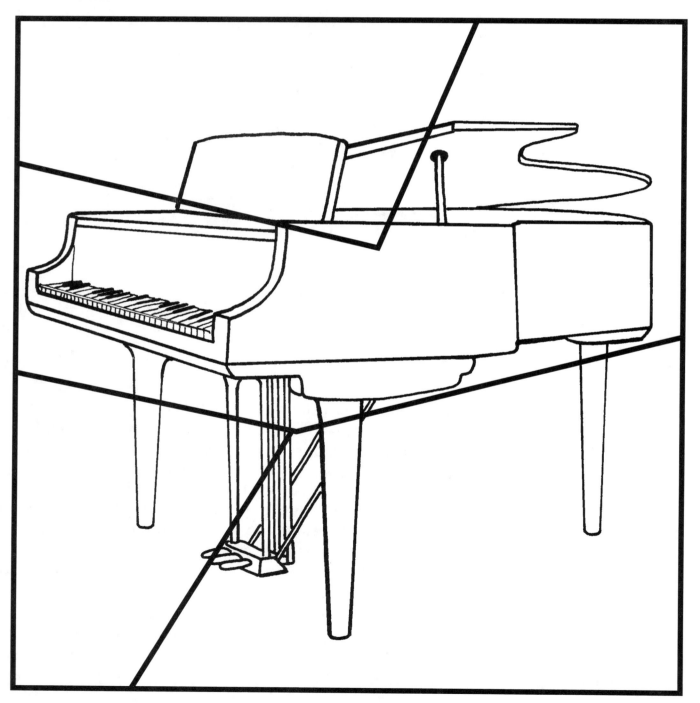

130

Talking Without Hearing

Ludwig van Beethoven lost his hearing. Today some of the people who cannot hear use their hands to talk. You can learn how to talk by spelling words with your hands.

Finger Spelling

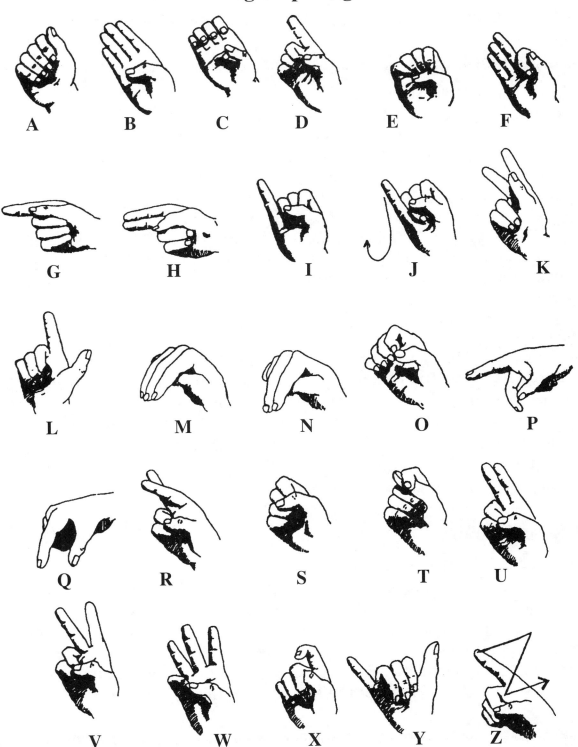

Music Appreciation Week

After completing the music unit, have students celebrate Music Appreciation Week using the activities on pages 132–135 or by creating some of your own.

Class Symphony

Gather instruments, such as hardwood blocks, 4-inch (10 cm) triangles, 6-inch (15 cm) triangles, wrist bells, finger castanets, sand blocks, ankle bells, rhythm sticks, and different types of drums. Be sure there are enough instruments for every student to have one. Stress to students that this activity is not a time for them to aimlessly bang on instruments. In addition to music skills, students will be practicing how to listen and follow directions.

Have students sit in a circle with the instruments on the floor in the center of the circle. Ask one student at a time to select an instrument. Have students name the instruments they have chosen. Ask them to play their instruments, one at a time. This will help reinforce students' association of the names of the instruments with their sounds.

Have students sing songs such as *Old McDonald Had a Farm; Hickory, Dickory, Dock;* or *Pop Goes the Weasel.* Ask them to play their instruments as they sing the songs. Remind them to play softly so that the singing can be heard over the instruments. After students have played the instruments for a while, have them pass their instruments to the persons sitting on their right. Regularly rotate the instruments in this manner to ensure that all students get to play the different kinds of instruments.

Musical Chairs

Arrange the chairs so that every student will have one to sit on when the music stops. Do not remove any of the chairs as in the traditional game of Musical Chairs. The purpose of this activity is to help students improve their listening skills rather than foster a feeling of competitiveness. Tell students that they must be sure to sit down when they hear the music stop. Remind them that everyone will have a place to sit. Point out that each time the music stops they will probably be sitting in a different chair.

Music Appreciation Week *(cont.)*

Kazoo Symphony

Provide kazoos or request that parents send kazoos for your class, one per student. Have students listen to nursery rhyme music and play their kazoos. You may wish to have half of the class sing the songs and the other half play their kazoos and then switch roles. Remind students to play their kazoos using the correct beat and tempo of the music.

To purchase kazoos, check instrument catalogues for ordering information.

CATALOGUE SUGGESTIONS

Hohner
P.O. Box 15035
Richmond, VA 23227
Phone: 1-804-798-4500

Peripole, Inc.
P.O. Box 146
Browns Mills, NJ 08015
Phone: 1-609-654-5555

Music Quilt

Have students make a quilt, using one of the ideas suggested below. Display the quilt in the hall or library.

- pictures of instruments
- pictures of composers
- pictures of conductors
- pictures of musicians
- pictures that tell the major events in a symphony's story, such as *The Sorcerer's Apprentice*
- photographs of students engaged in music activities
- pictures drawn by students showing them playing their favorite instruments
- pictures of different types of notes
- titles of books read aloud that are about music
- pictures of toy instruments

Music Appreciation Week *(cont.)*

Instruments from Around the World

Show instruments or pictures of instruments from other cultures. Have students compare/contrast the instruments they have studied with the instruments from other parts of the world. Ask students to tell which instruments they would like to hear played. If possible, invite guest musicians to play some instruments from different cultures. Ask students what they liked and disliked about those instruments.

Being Hearing Impaired

Have students experience the loss of hearing that Beethoven did. Ask them to wear earmuffs over their ears or carefully placed cotton balls inside their ears. Then allow students to listen to a musical instrument, such as the piano, by feeling the vibrations.

Ask students how they felt about the experience of not being able to hear very well. Have them imagine that they cannot hear anything. Ask them what they would miss the most about not being able to hear.

If possible, take students on a field trip to a school for hearing impaired students. Otherwise, invite a person who works at such a school to speak to your class.

Inventions

Explain to students what an invention is. Tell them that they are going to pretend to be inventors and create new instruments. Distribute drawing paper to students. Have them draw pictures of their inventions. Invite students to name the new instruments and tell something about them. Write the names and sentences describing the instruments on the students' papers. Have students share their inventions with the class. Encourage them to tell about their new instruments. You may need to ask questions to help them describe their instruments.

Bands

Invite different types of bands to play for your celebration. Check with local high schools to see what kinds of bands they have and if they would be available to give a performance for your class or school.

Music Appreciation Week *(cont.)*

Art Activities

Have students do an art activity using one of the suggestions below.

- Provide white construction paper, magazines, and glue to students. Ask students to cut out and glue down pictures of instruments to make collages.

- Have groups of students work together to make mobiles of the instruments (violin, flute, horn, drum, harp, banjo, tambourine, cymbals, xylophone) that they made during this unit. Suspend the mobiles from the ceiling.

- Have students write a language experience story about music. Write the story on chart paper. Have students draw or paint illustrations for the story. Display the story and illustrations on a bulletin board.

Movement Activities

Have students do a movement activity using one of the suggestions below.

- Play a variety of music for students. Invite them to dance to the beat and tempo of the music. Discuss how beat and tempo can set the mood for the music. Explain how feelings, such as happy, sad, and scared, can be reflected in the music. Ask students to describe the mood of different pieces of music.

- Invite a variety of dancers (ballet, folk, jazz, tap, etc.) to perform for your class. If possible have these artists teach some simple dance steps to students.

- Have students work together to develop a routine of exercises to be done with specific pieces of classical music. Have students complete one or more exercise routines each day.

- Play some marching music. First, have students clap to identify the beat. Then, have them march in place to the beat. Finally, play the music and have students march around the school. Remind them they must march to the correct beat. You may wish to invite older students to twirl batons as you march the procession around the school.

Bulletin Board Ideas

Use the bulletin board ideas suggested below or create some of your own. Patterns are provided on page 137 to make a quick and easy musical border or decorations.

COMPOSERS	CONDUCTORS	MUSICIANS

THE SOUNDS OF MUSIC

Bulletin Board Ideas *(cont.)*

Use the patterns shown below as a border or decorations for your music bulletin boards, including the ones suggested on page 136. Reproduce as many as you need and attach.

Parent Letter #1

Dear Parents,

Our class is studying about music. At school, we are using a variety of hands-on activities to learn about musical instruments and the careers of composers, conductors, and musicians. You can help your child learn about these topics by using the activities suggested below or by creating some of your own. Your help and support are greatly appreciated.

Suggested Activities:

- Listen to a recording of classical music with your child. Identify as many instruments as possible.

- Take your child to a variety of concerts so he or she has the opportunity to hear different types of music. Before attending a concert, discuss the jobs of composers, conductors, and musicians.

- Visit a local music store with your child. Discuss the different types of instruments that are on display.

- Encourage your child to show you the instruments that he or she made in class. Have your child pretend to play the instruments for you.

- Take your child to the public library. Together read books that are about music, instruments, composers, conductors, and/or musicians.

- Invite family members or friends to play musical instruments for you and your child.

Sincerely,

_____

Teacher

_____

School

Parent Letter #2

Dear Parents,

Our class is studying about the specific composers and pieces of music that are listed below. At school, we are using a variety of hands-on activities to learn about these composers and their music. You can reinforce what your child is learning at school by using the activities suggested below or by creating some of your own. Your help and support are greatly appreciated.

1. Sergei Prokofiev — *Peter and the Wolf*
2. Franz Joseph Haydn — *The Clock Symphony; The Surprise Symphony*
3. Leopold Mozart — *Toy Symphony*
4. Wolfgang Amadeus Mozart — Variations on the theme of *"Twinkle, Twinkle Little Star"*
5. Paul Dukas — *The Sorcerer's Apprentice*
6. Camille Saint-Saëns — *The Carnival of the Animals*
7. Nikolai Rimsky-Korsakov — *The Flight of the Bumblebee*
8. Ludwig van Beethoven — *Pastoral Symphony*

Suggested Activities:

- Read aloud the Little Books your child made at school.
- Ask your child to tell you about the activities we are doing at school.
- Encourage your child to show and explain his or her completed projects to family members and friends.
- If possible, get copies of the recordings from the public library or local music stores. Listen to them with your child and then discuss the music.

Sincerely,

_____
Teacher

_____
School

Invitations

Dear _____ ,

I am a teacher at _____ School.
My class is studying about music. To help the children learn more about musical instruments, I would like them to have the opportunity to see and listen to musicians. I sincerely hope that you will be able to share your musical talents with my class.

Please let me know whether you will be available to visit our class. Thank you for your time.

Sincerely,

_____
Teacher

_____
School

_____
Phone

Dear Parents,

Please join us for our Music Appreciation Day. We will be having a variety of activities that everyone is sure to enjoy. We hope you will be able to come to our celebration.

DATE: _____   TIME: _____

Sincerely,

_____
Teacher

_____
School

Thank You and Name Tags

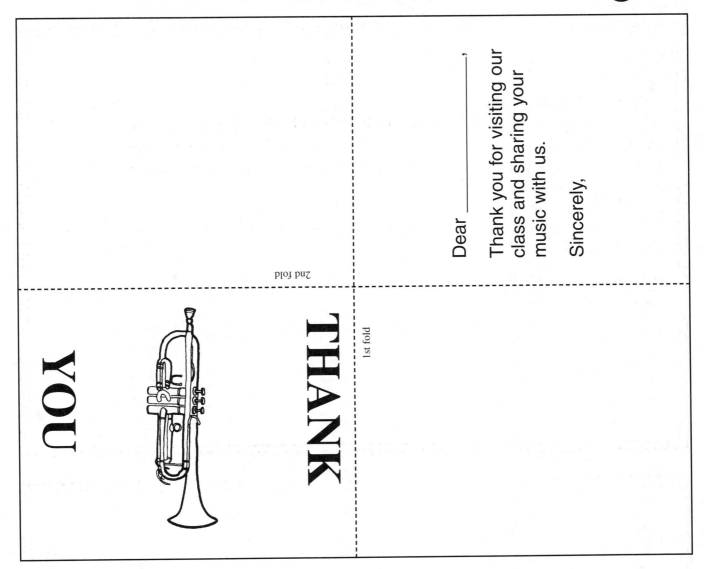

Dear _____,

Thank you for visiting our class and sharing your music with us.

Sincerely,

2nd fold

THANK

YOU

1st fold

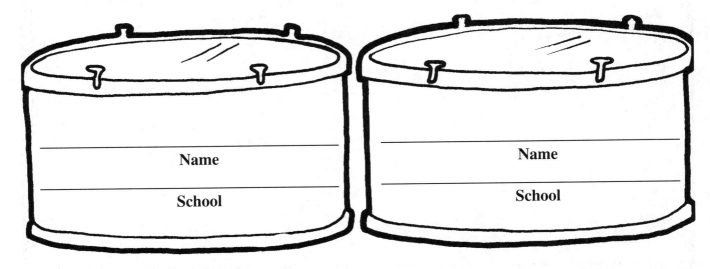

Name

School

Name

School

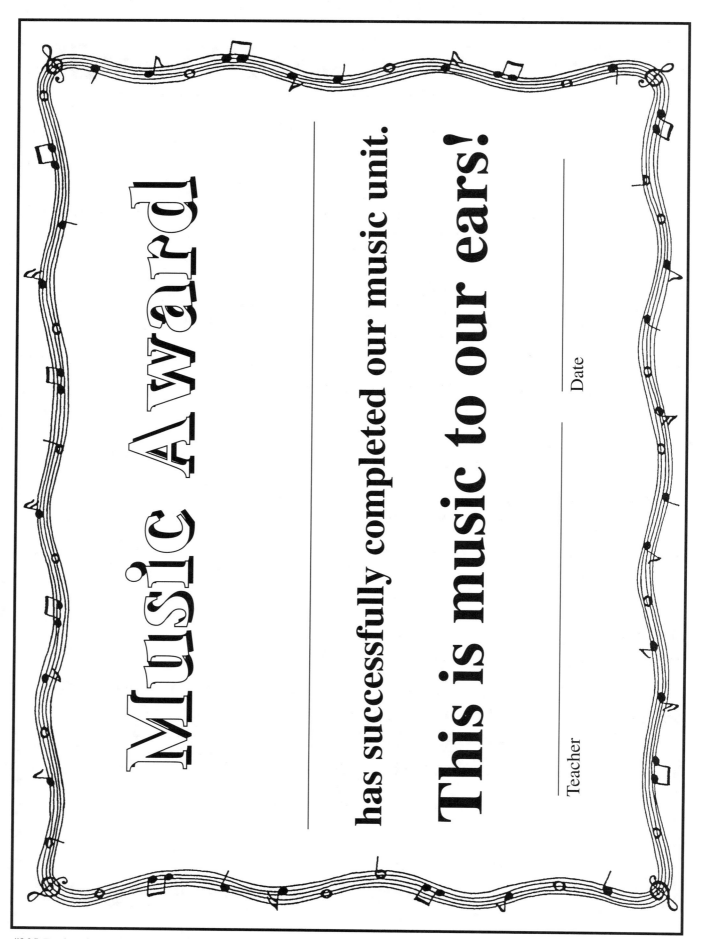

Music Award

has successfully completed our music unit.

This is music to our ears!

_____
Date

_____
Teacher

Technology Bibliography

Recordings

Obtain copies of the musical selections suggested for this unit from your school's music specialist, the public library, or local music stores.

Once Upon a Butterfly: A Narrated Musical Fantasy for Children. Carol Ann Eberle. Available from Heart to Heart Music.

Software

Beethoven: The String Quartet. (Includes rhythm meter, a time line, and glossary); CD-ROM for MAC; Available from Educorp, 7434 Trade St., San Diego, CA, 92121; 1-800-843-9497.

Brahms: A German Requiem. (Includes 50 biographical, historical, and musical references and 400 sound and music samples); CD-ROM for MAC; Available from Educorp, 7434 Trade St., San Diego, CA, 92121; 1-800-843-9497.

Microsoft Composer Collection. (Features the music of Mozart, Beethoven, and Schubert); CD-ROM for WIN; Microsoft; In the U.S. call 1-800-240-4782; In Canada call 1-800-563-9048.

Microsoft Musical Instruments. (Features over 200 instruments); CD-ROM for MAC or MPC; Microsoft; In the U.S. call 1-800-240-4782; In Canada call 1-800-563-9048.

Mozart: The Dissonant Quartet. (Features the Angeles Quartet); CD-ROM for MAC; Available from Educorp, 7434 Trade St., San Diego, CA, 92121; 1-800-843-9497.

The Orchestra. (Provides solos by each instrument in the orchestra); CD-ROM for MAC; Available from Educorp, 7434 Trade St., San Diego, CA, 92121; 1-800-843-8497.

Videos

Beethoven Lives Upstairs. The Children's Group Inc., 561 Bloor Street West, Suite 300, Toronto, Ontario, M55 1 Y6.

Fantasia. Walt Disney Home Video. Distributed by Buena Vista Home Video, Dept. CS, Burbank, CA, 91521.

The Orchestra. Mark Rubin Productions. Distributed by Music for Little People.

Peter and the Wolf. Walt Disney Home Video. Distributed by Buena Vista Home Video, Dept. CS, Burbank, CA, 91521.

Bibliography

Berger, Melvin. *The Science of Music.* Crowell, 1989.

Clary, Linday and Larry Harms. *Music for Little People.* Bradley Publications, 1985.

Collier, James Lincoln. *Duke Ellington.* Macmillan, 1991.

Collier, James Lincoln. *Louis Armstrong: An American Success Story.* Macmillan, 1985.

Cross, Milton and David Ewen. *The Milton Cross New Encyclopedia of The Great Composers and Their Music.* 2 Volumes. Doubleday, 1969.

Downing, Julie. *Mozart Tonight.* Bradbury, 1991.

Feierabend, John. *Music for Little People.* Boosey and Hawkes, 1989.

Feierabend, John. *Music for Very Little People.* Boosey and Hawkes, 1986.

Foster, Karen. *Rattles, Bells, and Chiming Bars.* Millbrook, 1992.

Greene, Carol. *John Philip Sousa: The March King.* Childrens Press, 1992.

Greene, Carol. *Ludwig van Beethoven: Musical Pioneer.* Childrens Press, 1989.

Greene, Carol. *Wolfgang Amadeus Mozart: Musical Genius.* Childrens Press, 1993.

Grimm, Jacob. *Bremen Town Musicians.* North South, 1992.

Hart, Avery and Paul Mantell. *Kids Make Music!* Williamson, 1993.

Hausherr, Rosemarie. *What Instrument Is This?* Scholastic, 1992.

Hautzig, Deborah. *Nutcracker Ballet.* Random, 1992.

Hautzig, Deborah. *Pied Piper of Hamlin.* Random, 1989.

Hayes, Ann. *Meet the Orchestra.* Harcourt Brace Jovanovich, 1991.

Hoffmann, E.T.A. *Nutcracker.* Picture Book, 1987.

Johnson, James Weldon. *Lift Every Voice and Sing.* Walker, 1993.

Krementz, Jill. *Very Young Musician.* Little Simon, 1991.

Krull, Kathleen. *Lives of the Musicians.* Harcourt, 1993.

Lemieux, Michelle. *Peter and the Wolf.* Morrow, 1991.

Musical Instruments. Scholastic, 1994.

Paker, Josephine. *Beating the Drum.* Millbrook, 1992.

Paker, Josephine. *Music from Strings.* Millbrook, 1992.

Paxton, Tom. *Animals' Lullaby.* Morrow, 1992.

Pillar, Marjorie. *Join the Band.* HarperCollins, 1992.

Prokofiev, Sergei. *Peter and the Wolf.* Picture Book, 1987.

Rosenberg, Jane. *Play Me a Story.* Knopf, 1994.

Staples, Danny. *Flutes, Reeds, and Trumpets.* Millbrook, 1992.

Stevens, Janet. *Bremen Town Musicians.* Holiday, 1992.

Tames, Richard. *Frederic Chopin.* Watts, 1991.

Tames, Richard. *Ludwig van Beethoven.* Watts, 1991.

Tames, Richard. *Peter Ilyich Tchaikovsky.* Watts, 1991.

Tames, Richard. *Richard Wagner.* Watts, 1991.

Törnqvist, Rita and Marit. *The Old Musician.* Rabén & Sjögren, 1993.

Van Kampen, Vlasta. *Orchestranimals.* Scholastic, 1989.

Weil, Lisl. *The Magic of Music.* Holiday, 1989.